LONELINESS
IS NOT A DISEASE

Tim Timmons

HARVEST HOUSE PUBLISHERS
Eugene, Oregon 97402

Except where otherwise indicated, all Scripture quotations in this book are taken from the New American Standard Bible, Copyright © The Lockman Foundation 1960, 1962, 1963, 1968, 1971, 1972, 1973, 1975. Used by permission.

LONELINESS IS NOT A DISEASE

Copyright © 1981 by Shasta Press

Published by Harvest House Publishers
Eugene, Oregon 97402

Library of Congress Catalog Card Number 80-83845
ISBN 0-89081-264-0

Printed in the United States of America.

SPECIAL ACKNOWLEDGMENTS

MARTHA KIMMELL GREENE for her research assistance.

JUDITH ANN WILSON for the extra hours of typing this manuscript and the helpful editorial assistance in preparation for publication.

KAREN LEE DAVISON for her laborious transcription work.

Tim Timmons has authored the following books:

Maximum Marriage

Ultimate Lifestyle

Game Plan for Marriage

Maximum Living in a Pressure-Cooker World

Tim Timmons has created over 100 hours of video and audio cassette tapes challenging people toward reality, relationships, and responsibility.

AUDIO TAPES:

Maximum Marriage — 6 hours
Maximum Parenthood — 6 hours
Ultimate Lifestyle — 6 hours
The Single Solution — 4 hours
Biblical Lovemaking — 4 hours
Maximum Manhood — 4 hours
Have We Been Fooled? — 8 hours
Maximum Living — 4 hours
The Family Connection — 10 hours

VIDEO TAPES:

Maximum Living in a Pressure-Cooker World — 4 hours
Maximum Lifestyle — 4 hours

DEDICATION

To my mother, Hilda Timmons, a terrific lady and a special mom, who died from the pain of loneliness.

INTRODUCTION

Many women have married because of loneliness, and years later have divorced for the same reason. Loneliness is everywhere and in everyone! There are no exceptions. Only the level of intensity of the pain of loneliness distinguishes us from one another. Everybody is lonely!

More people, their lives consisting of proximity without presence, are feeling lonely with relationships without contact, and familiarity without feeling. Too many people feel isolated—aimless, useless, and alienated. The sad truth about us human beings is that there are now more humans with less being than ever before. The spectrum of our condition may be wide and the symptoms legion, but there is only one root cause: *the absence of intimacy*.

When Bob Hawkins first challenged me to write about loneliness, I didn't realize to what extent I would be affected personally. I knew that loneliness was everywhere, but I believed it to be one of the many spin-off problems of egoism. But now I clearly understand that loneliness is not a spin-off problem. To the contrary, it is at the very core of most of the problems we face today. Depression, anxiety, anger, and guilt are a few of the popular masks worn by the real killer—*loneliness*.

The most therapeutic experience for me in researching and writing this book was when I was forced into a face-to-face confrontation with my own loneliness! A girl had tried to kill herself again through the use of pills. When I arrived on the scene, her mother was filling her full of coffee and she was slowly waking up. The girl said, "I'm just so lonely!" I quickly responded, "I know." She turned to me and said, "What do you know about loneliness?"

I found myself responding as a counselee being questioned by a counselor. I spilled my guts as I revealed my pain of loneliness to her. Much of the loneliness I admitted was a new realization to me as well! The loneliness I feel because of my only-child experiences, the pain from the loss of my father and mother, the aloneness experienced as a leader, and the loneliness from the distance I have created from time to time in my marriage are a few of the components of my pain of loneliness.

Later, as I reflected on my surprise confession of loneliness, I was able to realize what I had been doing with gnawing pain. Whenever my behavior was not proper or was even destructive in relationships, I blamed my anxious feelings on depression, anger, guilt, or a headache. But in reality it was none of the above. It was loneliness all along!

In admitting my loneliness I was able to pin it up on my psychological "wall" as a target. Through new insights into my loneliness and a few critical decisions based upon those insights, I have been amazed at the positive changes in my life! In addition to the inner confidence, I have experienced a new freedom of expression in all my relationships. It's like I have been interrelating with people (wife, children, friends) on only one channel of a four-channel system. Now I'm increasingly enjoying the communication flow on all four channels. I am eliminating my pain of loneliness through learning how to love more fully!

Man is essentially alone and lonely, and from this isolation he cannot be saved by someone else, but only by himself through the fact that he loves. It is the fear of love which is the root cause of every attitude and form of behavior that separates us from each other. We are lonely because of our fear of love. The fear of love is the foundational fear which underlies the fear of identity (the love of who you are), the fear of inadequacy (the fear of what you do), and the fear of intimacy (the love of others).

If loneliness were a disease savagely attacking human beings everywhere, then there would be little hope for a quick discovery of its cure. But loneliness is not a disease. It's a decision! It's a decision to avoid the fears of the pain which accompanies identity (companion pain of dissatisfaction), inadequacy (companion pain of depreciation), and intimacy (companion pain of detachment). Since loneliness is a decision and not a disease, there is hope! If a decision or series of decisions made me lonely, then a decision or series of decisions can relieve my loneliness. Inside loneliness is hope!

—Tim Timmons

CONTENTS

Introduction   9

PART ONE:
LONELINESS: A TASTE OF HELL!

1. Big Brother Isn't Watching   13
2. Middle-Age Crazy   27
3. Terrorism Within the Family   41
4. The Pain Can Kill You!   53
5. I'm Not O.K., You're Not O.K.,
   and That's O.K.   69

PART TWO:
LOVE: A TASTE OF HEAVEN!

6. Loneliness Is a Decision   81
7. Pseudolove   93
8. True Love   105
9. True Love: Release It!   117
10. From Loneliness to Love   139

   Appendix

I. Perfect Love   147
II. When You Need a Faith Lift   157

PART ONE

Loneliness: A Taste of Hell!

1

Big Brother Isn't Watching

Big Brother isn't watching—he'd rather be alone! Perhaps what distinguishes the modern family from its colonial counterpart is its new-found privacy. Throughout the seventeenth and eighteenth centuries, well over 90 percent of the American population lived in small, rural communities. Unusual behavior rarely went unnoticed, and neighbors often intervened directly in a family's affairs, to help or to chastise.[1] But the tight boundaries of rural, neighborhood, family-centered America have

---

[1]All notes are listed at the back of this book.

burst, breaking the bonds of exclusiveness and duty and freeing people for alternatives that seem to have no end. And yet—there is the problem of loneliness.[2]

The privacy that distinguishes the modern family from its colonial counterpart carries a high pricetag—*loneliness*. It's everywhere! There are no exemptions. Loneliness knows no boundaries. Everyone experiences loneliness to some degree—the rich and the poor, the employed and the unemployed. Adults and children, men and women, married and single. Leaders and followers. God-fearing people, agnostics, and atheists. The intelligent and the not-so-intelligent. People in a crowd and people all alone. Without exception, if you have a pulse, you experience loneliness!

Masks of Loneliness

Loneliness is the single experience most common to all of us, yet it is the most misunderstood.[3] Loneliness most frequently masquerades in the many costumes it creates— depression, anger, guilt, poor self-image, suicide, psychological anxiety, physical illnesses, etc. Loneliness is so elusive. It's an ache of quiet desperation that escapes identification. Loneliness refuses to speak for itself, but instead uses the identification and symptoms of every other available problem.

Until recently, loneliness has escaped the attention and focus it deserves for being the culprit impregnating nearly every kind of psychological problem that man faces. Erich Fromm in his insightful book *The Art of Loving* zeroes in on loneliness as located at the core of man's existence: "The deepest need of man is the need to overcome his separateness, to leave the prison of his aloneness."[4] Norman Cousins in an essay entitled *Modern Man is Obsolete* expresses the same concept a little differently: "All man's history is an endeavor to shatter his loneliness."[5]

The Loneliness Vacuum

Loneliness is an inner vacuum—a capacity that craves to be filled and satisfied. This vacuum is most clearly felt during times of loss of loved ones. A significant love relationship can be lost through death, divorce, marital separation, or the all-too-frequent uprooting of the family for the greener grass on the other side of a new fence. The American family is so shattered by all of the above that only one out of six families is considered normal (husband and wife in their first marriage with children). The fragmented family is now the norm; 38 percent of all first marriages will end in divorce, and 79 percent of those people will marry again. There were over one million divorces last year, and there will be even more this year. The family continues to fall apart.

It's no wonder that the inner vacuum of loneliness is so prevalent in our society!

Loneliness: Inside the Family Connection

Logically speaking, the least likely place for loneliness would seem to be in a setting where people live together under the same roof—in marriage and the family. This is in line with the myth that loneliness means being without people. But in our society, loneliness is most rampant inside the family connection. Isn't it true that we expect more from family members in the way of understanding? When this does not happen, our loneliness can be severe. The intensity of our reactions to people is in direct proportion to the degree of our expectations. If we expect an acquaintance to understand us but find that he doesn't, we may be disappointed. But when a member of our own immediate family has misunderstood us, our loneliness can plunge down to its most painful level.[6]

Loneliness lurks around the relationship with the most potential for intimacy. In the 14-year-old marriage in which the ache of aloneness is gnawing away at the very threads that hold them together, the loneliness is unidentified, but its destruction is very real just the same. Then there is the 20-year-old marriage in which husband and wife wake up to an empty nest, the pain of loneliness, and apparently nothing left to ease the pain or fill the vacuum . . . or the newlyweds who find that their relationship was built upon wrong foundations or unrealistic expectations, and so feel like roommates . . . or the parent's pain of loneliness caused by the deafening silence of a child who will not truly communicate any longer . . . or the exhausted woman who longs to be her husband's lover and not just the mother of his children . . . or the longtime friendship ripped apart because you were misunderstood . . . or the nausea and frustration of the inability to penetrate the many surface relationships of the everyday crowd in your world . . . or the "happily married" "successful" executive who feels dissatisfaction with the prison of his life . . . or the child who desperately wants to reveal his feelings with mom or dad but is afraid to open up too far . . . or the longing of anyone, anywhere, who desires to be understood by someone who cares.

More people are feeling lonely; their lives consist of proximity without presence, relationships without contact, and familiarity without feeling. Too many people feel isolated—aimless, useless, and alienated. The sad truth about us human beings is that there are now more *humans* with less *being* than ever before. The spectrum of our condition may be wide and the symptoms legion, but there is only one root cause: *the absence of intimacy*.[7]

Vacuum Stuffers: Groups and Gurus

The conventional ways of forming relationships no longer work in contemporary urban society. To fill the void left by conventional methods of beginning and continuing relationships, a new multibillion-dollar service industry has grown up in America. Encounter groups, growth-and-awareness centers, singles apartment complexes, bars and clubs, pseudoreligious and mystical groups—all have flourished either entirely or partially because of the need of Americans today to find relationships that will help them fill their loneliness vacuum.[8]

When openness and honesty fail to achieve their stated aim—a significant relationship—then comes a possible last resort: absorption in one of the various spiritual pseudoreligions led by any number of gurus who roam the world in search of lonely followers.[9] Through the encounter groups and mass therapies these followers have tried listening to themselves and their own inner voices, and that hasn't worked. So they may decide to listen to others for a change, to people who will tell them what to do and who to be. And so we have the birth of new gods—gurus whose mystical charisma promises a magical union and an escape from one's loneliness.[10]

Experts Legalize Hugging

Emotional support that once came from families, neighbors, friends, ministers, rabbis, and priests is now purchased from psychiatrists, psychologists, and various social service agencies—the experts! While delivering needed support to people, these "experts" have also tended to usurp our functions and relieve us of our sense of personal responsibility. The "experts" have raped us of our confidence in directing our own lives.[11]

What a commentary on our society! Adults feel the need to relieve their loneliness by going to scientific institutes and relying on scientific "experts" to legitimize human intimacy. Equally remarkable and ironic is the fact that scientific "experts" feel they have the "scientific data" that makes behavior like hugging legal. We have come to the point where adults have to play the legalized, childish games of touch-and-hug in order to find a thread of intimacy.[12]

The Big "I"

The "experts" place excessive importance on self-progression. Under the banner of the self-help movement people are becoming more self-centered and selfish. It's nothing more than an "optical" problem—the "I". People are so into themselves without interconnecting with other people that isolation and loneliness are inevitable. Families everywhere are being ripped apart by people attempting to "find" themselves in isolation—severing longtime relationships in order to go chase themselves, alone. Interrelatedness as a solution is so far from the experts' priorities that much of the self-help movement intensifies the pain of loneliness rather than easing it.

The Encounter Prophet's Prayer is a good example of this emphasis on the big "I" and the de-emphasis on relationships:

> I do my own thing, and you do your
> own thing.
> I am not in this world to live up to your
> expectations
> And you are not in this world to live
> up to mine.
> You are you and I am I,
> And if by chance we find each
> other, it's beautiful.
> If not, it can't be helped.[13]

The solution to loneliness offered by the loneliness business—mass therapies, the singles industry, much of the self-help movement, the "experts," and the guru or new-religious movements—often exploits people's sense of alienation and depression rather than resolving it. The primary aim of most of the loneliness business is profit and power over others. The dangers and failures of the loneliness business are far more numerous than its successes. On both the social and personal levels the boundaries of the self are either reduced or totally eliminated. In the name of privacy and individual freedom, people's personal lives, their emotions, and their human needs are transformed into commodities whose price tags can be prohibitive. Human-relations skills replace relationships, and private emotions are manipulated in the service of industrial profit.[14]

Alone is not Lonely

In Genesis it says that it is not good for man to be alone, but sometimes aloneness is a great relief! Alone is not lonely. To be alone is a physical separation, whereas to be lonely is a psychological and spiritual separation. To be lonely is not only to be solitary, for you can choose to be alone. To be lonely also means to feel cut off from other people, isolated and alienated. Loneliness is a killer.[15]

It is said that solitude is a good place to visit but a poor place to stay. Later we will see how important it is to be alone. May Sarton, in her *Journal of a Solitude*, reveals the virtue of being alone: "I am here alone for the first time in weeks, to take up my 'real' life again at last. That is what is strange—that friends, even passionate loves, are not my real life unless there is time alone which to explore and to discover what is happening or has happened."[16]

Being alone in the good sense of the word is a rarity in our world today. In America we have become masters of the "surfacy" relationship. There is so much contact with people without the time to penetrate beyond the surface. Some say that when you become used to never being alone, you have become Americanized.

In fact, we have developed a phobia of being alone; we prefer the most trivial and even obnoxious company, the most meaningless activities, to being alone with ourselves; we seem to be frightened at the prospect of facing ourselves. Is it because we feel we would be such bad company? I think the fear of being alone with ourselves is instead a feeling of embarrassment which sometimes borders on terror at seeing a person at the same time so well-known and so strange, so we are afraid and run away.[17]

There is a difference between *existential loneliness* (which is a reality of being human, of being aware, and of facing ultimate experiences of upheaval, tragedy, and change, the intrinsic loneliness of being born, of living at the extremes, of dying) and the *anxiety of loneliness* (which is not true loneliness but is a defense that attempts to eliminate it by constantly seeking activity, either with others or else by continually keeping busy to avoid facing the crucial questions of life and death). Existential loneliness (with many variations) expresses itself in two basic forms: the *loneliness of solitude* (a peaceful state of being alone with the ultimate mystery of life—people, nature, the universe) and the *loneliness of a broken life* (a life suddenly shattered by betrayal, deceit, rejection, gross misunderstanding, pain, separation, illness, death, tragedy, and crisis that severely alter not only one's sense of self but the world in which one lives—one's relationships and work projects).[18]

Being alone or being lonely is all part of the human condition. It's a universal truth. Everyone will be physically alone and everyone experiences psychological loneliness.

Excuses for Loneliness

Although everybody experiences loneliness, very few people have been willing to admit it. Either loneliness is flatly denied or it is artfully excused. It's a con game that people play—a self-con!

The many masks and disguises of loneliness have become such acceptable faces to all of us that they have become like second skins—second skins that insulate us comfortably and efficiently. These skins themselves are the excuses used to avoid confrontation with the reality of loneliness.[19] There is the skin of independence/freedom. Here the excuse is that any loneliness you experience is the price tag for independence and freedom. There is also the common skin of strength and toughness. The excuse used by this skin is that for you to admit loneliness is a sign of weakness. Therefore deny it! For most people the first step toward alleviating the pain of loneliness will be literally to jump out of their skins!

Over the past few decades our society has refined a response to human loneliness that can be described as a cultural pact of ignorance. This is a peculiar type of conspiracy in which some of the victims of loneliness are the perpetrators of their own suffering. The conspiracy involves a subtle denial of certain aspects of loneliness. In spite of all the talk about loneliness, the word "loneliness" often seems to be completely detached from feelings, and especially detached from the idea that it involves suffering. ("If you don't tell me you are suffering from loneliness, then I won't tell you I am suffering either.")

With the meanings of words changed or impoverished, the impression is created that loneliness is no longer really an issue; no one is really suffering—everyone is liberated and free to do his or her own thing. Anyone who wants a "relationship" can have one, and that's cool; in fact *everything* is cool. Many lonely people do not appear to be lonely at all—they do not look like they are suffering—and so the truly lonely individual is forced to believe that he is the only one suffering and therefore shouldn't talk about it. We live in a society in which King Loneliness has no clothing, yet because everyone believes that he is the only person who feels lonely, we tell ourselves that loneliness must be a mirage.[20]

Our common plight is that it is becoming increasingly difficult to share the most basic of all human truths: that people desperately need each other, that we really are dependent on one another. Instead, many people console themselves with cliches such as "I'm O.K. so you must be O.K." while all the time they are not O.K. Feelings of isolation are massaged by slogans that only serve to make people all the more lonely. In a conspiracy of silence about their true loneliness, people deceive each other, and so make loneliness and isolation all the more prevalent.[21]

Loneliness is everywhere! It's like an invisible ghost that haunts people everywhere. Loneliness may be denied, excused, or unnoticed, but it will never be handled effectively without calling it what it is and attacking it effectively.

2

Middle-Age Crazy

"Sometimes I sit in my apartment all alone. And I think of the rent I'm paying. And it's crazy! But then, it's what I always wanted. My own apartment, a car, and plenty of women. And still . . . I'm lonely" (Happy Loman, *Death of a Salesman* by Arthur Miller).

It *is* crazy! Some have called it "middle-age crisis," but without a doubt the most appropriate tag ever used to describe most of our society's behavior pattern is "middle-age crazy."

Information Bombardment

We are all being driven a little crazy by our swirling society. The spark of loneliness within each person is formed by this swirl of bombardments. *Information bombardment* produces overstimulation of the mind and psyche, and over a period of time results in our emotional earthquake—a kind of snapping. The threat of

snapping extends far beyond America's re-
ligious cults and mass therapies, beyond their
dramatic rituals and intense experiences to the
overwhelming pressures of less-immediately-
observable changes in awareness, as well a sudden and drastic alterations of personality. Just as
moving land masses may shift gradually and
imperceptibly, and then give way in a massive
earthquake, so too the sheer mass and movement of experience—of information—that has
engulfed our culture in recent years may bring
about changes in individual personalities,
making us less aware, more vulnerable to
manipulation, and ultimately less than fully
capable of thinking and acting as human
beings. The forces are bombarding each of us
daily and are becoming more intense.[1]

This flood of information and experience
makes up the constant, comprehensive assault
on human awareness that confronts most
Americans each day. Yet the more experience
an individual consumes—the more information he tries to process—the more confused he
may become, causing his mind to become dis-
jointed, scattered, unguarded, and vulnerable
to suggestion. Many cults make use of this
principle when they concoct exotic ritual environments combining strange music, lights,
incense, and foreign languages which may
confuse and eventually control the potential
convert's awareness. This same principle of
distraction, however, can be found in

countless everyday forms: in television commercials that use beautiful models to confuse the viewer's desires, or in extravagant supermarket displays that bombard the senses with dozens of competing brands of the same product. These effects are deliberately subtle and are designed to be gazed upon just long enough to slip some message or suggestion past our normally more attentive decision-making processes.[2]

There are three distinct varieties of information disease in America today. The most prevalent is the *sustained altered state of awareness*. The altered state is not one of enlightenment or mind expansion but is the state of narrowed or reduced awareness which is clearly visible among many of America's young cult members. Then there is the *delusional phase*. This second variety of information disease is characterized by an absence of feeling and emotion. It may result in vivid hallucinations and even irrational, violent, and self-destructive behavior. The third variety of information disease takes the form of *not thinking*, of shutting off the mind, and can result in the complete dissolution of personality. This state is common among cult members and practitioners of many self-help therapies, and it is the most damaging of the three varieties. Lonely people are caught in the swirl of information bombardment and the resulting identity confusion.[3]

Choice Bombardment

Another contributing factor to the massive identity confusion is the bombardment of choice. In scrambling for a way to a meaningful life, we find paradoxically an abundance of choices marked by an increased sense of loss of freedom.[4] Never before has such freedom of choice been available in regard to work, styles of life, and beliefs. Youth may well be victims of the dilemma of overchoice.[5]

This kind of pressure can lead to a point where people will no longer even try to make decisions. In his perceptive account of the changes wrought in our lives by technology, Alvin Toffler comments in *Future Shock:* "The society of the future will consist of adults who opt out of choice . . . who let others make decisions for them."[6]

Choice bombardment produces the pressure of *overcommitment*, and it will turn you every which way but loose! Commitments related to marriage, family, vocation, friends, church, community, and leisure all vie for your attention. There are so many "good" things to choose from that there is little or no time left for the "best" things. Rather than actively living life on purpose, most people wind up in a reactionary stance—living life accidentally and psychologically alone.

Choice bombardment invades our lives most intensively through the media. This well-oiled machinery of mass persuasion assumes and operates on the robot model of man. It pours out a constant flow of information to the American public designed to stimulate the consumer's guilts, fears, weaknesses, insecurities, and fantasies, and then it rewards each individual with immediate mental and emotional gratification for succumbing to them. Television may also be a potent neutralizing force of human thought and feeling. Its incessant transmission of information physically trains an individual to hear and observe without stopping to think, to switch from one set of sounds and images to the next without pausing to reflect or digest the information he has consumed.[7]

Not only does the bombardment cause identity confusion, but it forces people to create the shells, skins, and masks used to keep everything "out" and away from the real person.

Antihuman Bombardment

Still another contributing factor to identity confusion is the bombardment of antihuman influences. Antihuman bombardment produces a sense of *detachment* in personal relationships. It is a flight from feeling! For many reasons, personal relations have become increasingly risky—most obviously, because they no longer carry any assurance of permanence.[8] Arising out of a pervasive dissatisfaction with the quality of personal relations, the consciousness movement advises people not to make too large an investment in love and friendships, to avoid excessive dependence on others, and to live for the moment— the very conditions that created the crisis of personal relations in the first place.[9]

As social life becomes more and more warlike and barbaric, personal relations (which ostensibly provide relief from these conditions) take on the character of combat. Some of the new therapies dignify this combat as "assertiveness" and "fighting fair in love and marriage." Others celebrate impermanent attachments under such formulas as "open marriage" and "open-ended commitments." Thus they intensify the problem they pretend to solve.[10]

Detachment caused by antihuman bombardment permeates where we work as well as where we live. While modern industry condemns people to jobs that insult their intelligence, the mass culture of romantic escape fills their heads with visions of experience beyond their means (as well as beyond their emotional and imaginative capacities) and thus contributes to a further devaluation or routine. The disparity between romance and reality, the world of the beautiful people and the workaday world, gives rise to an ironic detachment that dulls pain but also cripples the will to change social conditions, to make even modest improvements in work and play, and to restore meaning and dignity to everyday life.[11]

Not only is there detachment from reality and relationships, but also from the very fiber of the human being—his or her personness. Any job becomes a threat to me if it stifles all search and swallows up my individuality, making me indistinguishable from any other cog in society's machine. In such a situation, the job refashions the man, and all that is left for him is never to act but only to react.[12]

Loneliness Escape Attempts

Lonely people are swept up in mass escape from the detachment, in overcommitment, and in overstimulation of the pressure-cooker world. They are a product of the futile attempt on the part of millions of Americans to avoid the responsibilities of being human in this difficult, threatening age.[13]

The mass escape is a psychological strategy for controlling and escaping from strong feeling. Many prefer the escape of drugs, while others simply undertake to live alone. The rising rate of suicide among young people can be attributed, in part, to a flight from emotional entanglements. As a matter of fact, we are all, in one form or another, attempting to develop a psychological strategy for escaping from the strong feelings produced by this pressure-cooker world! The most obvious result is the universal problem of loneliness.[14]

All the world has become a perpetual earthquake, and we have all been left with our feet firmly planted in midair! That which used to provide us with stability isn't around anymore. We have lost the past (history) by which we learn and form tradition. And we have lost the future (hope) by which we dream and make plans. Both are necessary for building and maintaining stability. Today we have limited ourselves to the immediate—the *now!* We have developed a perverted sense of history, with no thought for the future. Instant enjoyment is the goal. When I don't get what I want immediately, I either throw things or opt out. I revolt. That work takes time, that healing is rarely immediate or perfect, that growth is gradual, that reform may be a long process—these ideas are far removed from our modern mentality. What matters is that we have what we want, and that we have it now! But if that doesn't work, then the move into loneliness is a "safe" retreat.[15]

Narcissism: Going Crazy in a Hurry!

Every age develops its own peculiar forms of pathology, which express in exaggerated form its underlying character structure. Ours is the age of narcissism, recalling the Greek legend about the beautiful youth who fell in love with his reflection in a pool and pined away in rapture over it.[16]

Narcissism is a combination of an exaggerated sense of self-importance and a lack of sustained positive regard for others. A narcissist isn't really in love with himself—self-hatred is more prevalent than self-love. Narcissists actually have low opinions of themselves, and that is why they constantly seek approval. They consider themselves unworthy and unlovable, so they attempt to hide those feelings by getting the outside world to proclaim them extraordinary or unique. Even then they suffer from intense, unconscious envy that makes them want to degrade, depreciate, and spoil what others have and they lack, particularly others' capacity to love and give. The narcissist is never totally satisfied by what he receives from others, and he usually ends up feeling frustrated and empty.[17]

Incapable of loving themselves, narcissists cannot give to their partners in a relationship. The capacity to fall in love implies the ability to idealize another person. In a sense, all love begins as infatuation. Initially we see the loved one as extraordinary, remarkable, even perfect, but inevitably as the relationship continues things begin to look different, and disappointment sets in. When people are in love, they regenerate the feeling of idealization again and again over a long period of time, but the narcissist can't idealize anyone for very long. As soon as a person whom the narcissist has idealized responds to him, that person loses his or her value. The narcissist is purely exploitive in his relationships with other people. It's as if he were squeezing a lemon and dropping the remains.[18]

The narcissistic personality disorder has become such a widespread problem in our society that it received official clinical status in the American Psychiatric Association's diagnostic manual in 1980. The description reads:

A. Grandiose sense of self-importance.

B. Preoccupation with fantasies of unlimited success, power, brilliance, beauty, or ideal love.

C. Exhibitionistic: requires constant attention and admiration.

D. Responds to criticism, indifference of others, or defeat with either cool indifference or with marked feelings of rage, inferiority, shame, humiliation, or emptiness.

E. At least two of the following are characteristic of disturbances in interpersonal relationships:

1. Lack of empathy: inability to recognize how others feel.

2. Entitlement: expectation of special favors without assuming reciprocal responsibilities.

3. Interpersonal exploitiveness.

4. Relationships characteristically vacillate between the extremes of overidealization and devaluation.[19]

Narcissism: Crazy with Rage

As previously mentioned, narcissism is not just a synonym for selfishness. It is more than that. Narcissism is intricately connected to our fast-paced, confused society and the pressure cooker of rage that builds within. The narcissist tends to cultivate a protective shallowness in emotional relations. He lacks the capacity to mourn, because the intensity of his rage against love objects, in particular against his parents, prevents his reliving happy experiences or treasuring them in memory. Sexually promiscuous rather than repressed, he nevertheless finds it difficult to elaborate the sexual impulse or to approach sex in the spirit of play. Instead, sex is a drive or rage! He avoids close involvements because they might release intense feelings of rage. His personality consists largely of defenses against his rage. He conforms to social rules more out of fear of punishment than from a sense of guilt.[20]

The new narcissist is haunted not by guilt but by anxiety. His sexual attitudes are permissive rather than puritanical, even though his freedom from ancient taboos brings him no sexual peace. He extols cooperation and teamwork while harboring deeply antisocial impulses. He praises respect for rules and regulations in the secret belief that they do not apply to himself. Acquisitive in the sense that his cravings have no limits, he does not accumulate goods and provisions against the future, but demands immediate gratification and lives in a state of restless, perpetually unsatisfied desire.[21]

Almost all the relationships that antagonistic, hostile people attempt are characterized by quick boredom. Although they may form dramatic and overwhelming attachments, they are usually short-lived because each has little emotionally and nothing intellectually to give the other person. Often they victimize others sexually, and their quick, intense, often-frenetic physical activity peaks and cools, repeating itself in a consistently erratic pattern that provides nothing upon which to build a relationship. Always seeking excitement, they prowl constantly, looking for a situation in which their hostile behavior is appropriate. They believe that the world is against them, that people are no good, that honesty and hard work are for suckers, and that the road is too long and the path is too steep. They will promise anything, but because they have no involvement, promises and commitments are meaningless to them.[22]

Their single-minded devotion to what they do, their complete disregard for the feelings and rights of others, and their ability to become involved with people only as they can exploit them may help these people gain power and wealth. A few lonely people who never gain human involvement, love, or respect do succeed in gaining wealth or power through their total disregard for others and their total involvement with their own behavior. For each one who succeeds, however, thousands of others fail. Involved with their hostile behavior and without wealth and power, they lead a life of misery, frequently becoming alcoholics or drug addicts in order to reduce their pain.[23]

3

Terrorism Within the Family

A study by the University of Rhode Island concluded that the most dangerous place to be in the United States outside of riots and war is the American home! Although exact statistics are difficult to obtain, all the available studies have echoed the same sad story. The home is filled with anger and violence! Thirty percent of all American couples experience some form of domestic violence in their lifetime, and two million couples have used a gun, knife, or other lethal weapon on each other during their marriage. Twenty percent of all police officers killed in the line of duty are killed while answering calls involving family fights, and it is estimated that anywhere from six to fifteen million women are battered in the United States each year! As one law officer expressed it: "This is probably the highest unreported crime in the country."[1]

The real criminal is loneliness. Loneliness is a terrorist which rips families apart, leaving irreparable psychological wreckage and debris. Regrettably, the relational detachment of loneliness has hit the most basic unit of society—the family. The family's struggle to conform to an externally imposed ideal of family solidarity and parenthood creates an appearance of solidarity at the expense of spontaneous feeling, a ritualized "relatedness" empty of real substance. Because of the terrorism of loneliness, family relationships are forced into empty rituals.[2]

Giant Shock Absorber

The family is society's "giant shock absorber"—the place where bruised and battered individuals can retreat and rest after doing battle with the world, the one stable point in this ever-swirling confusion of society. But the superindustrial revolution has unfolded and exploded its time bombs; the giant "shock absorber" has been getting some shocks of its own.[3]

The family cycle has been a major sanity-preserving constant throughout human existence, and especially since the mass society has evolved. Today this cycle is accelerating—people grow up sooner, leave home sooner, marry sooner, and have children sooner. They space their children closer together and shorten their time of parenthood. In the words of Dr. Bernice Neugarten, a University of

Chicago specialist on family development, "The trend is toward a more rapid rhythm of events through most of the family cycle."[4]

All (Alone) in the Family

Most families begin with a marriage, and the dynamics of the marital relationship then set the pace and create the atmosphere for the family to come. Everyone, man and woman, is seeking personal fulfillment and expression in life—to love and be loved, to respect and be respected, to understand and be understood. Everyone is looking for a thread of relationship that penetrates through the surface to the warmth of intimacy. This search for closeness in a relationship is a survival search in order to ease the pain of loneliness. Actually it is not marriage that is critical in fending off the loneliness of emotional isolation but rather the availability of emotional attachment, of a relationship with another person such that the mere proximity of the other person can promote feelings of security and well-being.[5]

Unfortunately, the vast majority of marriages today are caught up in a "nonplan." The theme of this nonplan is offered often, and free of charge, by well-meaning friends and neighborhood marriage counselors: "It'll all work out!" It sounds easy enough! The only catch is that it doesn't work! This nonplan for marital bliss is based upon a competitive and comparative struggle which revolves around the question, "Who is more qualified here—you or me?"

Man: *Just the Family Paycheck*

When the man first asks himself this question, his initial response is, "Well, *I* am. I call most of the shots around here, and therefore I'm more qualified!" Then one day he comes home a little early and enters his castle during the "pit hour"—from 4:30 until the children are in bed. The kids have moved to the kitchen because their stomachs told them, "Move into the kitchen!" They have opened the refrigerator, spilled milk and juice, and dropped cookie crumbs. They have a peanut butter sandwich half made by the time mom realizes what's happening. She is swatting bottoms and threatening lives. Pets also descend upon the kitchen. The bird chirps louder. We have dogs and cats we have never met before hanging around during the "pit hour!"

In the middle of this chaos the man arrives home. With kids screaming, pets howling, the bathwater running, and dinner somewhere in between, he begins to feel incapable of exerting a controlling influence over the situation. Now he is not so sure about his shots. His wife seems to be surviving, but all he seems to be is ready to return to the office.

The man has heard the rumor that he's supposed to be the "head of the home." So one day he arrives home and announces to his family, "I am the head!" His wife doesn't believe him, the kids don't bat an eye, and not even the dog barks back! Having received such an overwhelming vote, the man retreats! However, the rumor is so prevalent that he returns and once again makes his announcement, this time with more hesitancy: "I am the head! Aren't I? How about when you're out shopping? Could I be the head then?" Now he's thoroughly confused.

Because of his confusion about what his responsibility should be in the home, the man decides to retreat to his office. In a sense he marries his business, and says, "You take care of the home. I'll deposit, you can withdraw, and then we'll have a dynamic marital relationship!"

Not long after the man has retreated from his responsibilities in the home, he begins to resent his wife for taking over in various household matters. He's the one who retreated, all right, but now he resents her, and his resentment turns into reaction. During crisis situations he says, "Why didn't you check with me before you did that? Didn't you even think to consult me about this, or have you even had a thought lately?"

The man is seeking total fulfillment—a full expression of himself as a person. Since he's retreated to the office and now resents his wife for taking over at home, he can't experience this fulfillment or expression with her, so he runs elsewhere. His business and other people then become substitutes for his relationship with his wife. The husband's retreat from his responsibility in the home is the most severely damaging move toward splitting and splintering the family.

But why is the man retreating from his responsibilities in the home? He is running from his family. He is desperately trying to find an intimate relationship to fill his vacuum of loneliness. He hasn't found it with his wife. He's worried, but painfully lonely. He needs to belong to someone. He wants his wife to be on his team, to empathize and understand him. Instead, he feels like an impersonal, unappreciated paycheck!

Woman: *Just a Maid, Cook, Governess, and Roommate*

The woman has heard a rumor too! She's heard that she is supposed to be her husband's "helpmate." However, this concept is normally presented as "helpmate equals doormat!" So the wife is out to prove herself more qualified than a doormat. This brings about all kinds of excitement and provides for all kinds of entertainment in the home. It becomes a two-ring circus. The man is announcing himself as the head and the woman is trying to prove herself more qualified than a doormat!

The woman's first response to the man's retreat from the home is to release him from his responsibilities there (he's just in the way most of the time anyway). However, as the pressures build up, she begins to resent her husband for not being there when she needs him. Her reaction during crisis situations is, "Where were you when I needed you? If you'd only be the man of the house, this kind of thing would never happen!"

Just like the man, the woman is seeking total fulfillment—a full expression of herself as a person. She certainly isn't experiencing a full expression of herself with her husband. In fact, it seems more like a full suppression, so she reacts. "Where were you when I needed you?" "Where have you ever been when I needed you?" "When I need you, you're never here!" "When I don't need you, here you are!"

Like her husband, she hasn't found even a thread of a relationship. She feels the ache of aloneness in her marriage. She is frustrated and suspects that she is worthless and unlovable. She is also living in quiet desperation—the pain of loneliness. She needs to belong to her husband, but is viewed as just the maid, the cook, the governess, and a roommate. For survival she runs elsewhere for some kind of respect and appreciation—to her children, to women's activities, to a vocation, to anywhere away from the hollow feeling of loneliness that she feels with her husband.

Child: Orphaned by His Parents

Following the model of his parents, the child quickly becomes a pro in competitive and comparative relationships. Each family member is on his own, because his parents have refused to communicate with him. He'll communicate about necessary and surface things like "Pass the butter," "May I have some money, mom?" or "Could you take me to the game?" But rarely will he communicate on the gut level and share what he's thinking or feeling on the inside.

A noncommunicative relationship inevitably brings about resentment and rebellion. Parents usually react to this rebellion with a new list of regulations, and yet even though that's the most natural response, it also turns out to be the most disastrous! More regulations without a healthy relationship only produce more rebellion.

As soon as he can, the child runs elsewhere, from an insecure base at home to an even more insecure society. He's searching for the fulfillment that he missed in his family relationships. He's out to fill up all the gaps and vacuums of loneliness that he senses inside, and he'll try it all until he finds something that fits. He's been orphaned emotionally by his parents and launched into a race of running—running frantically from his loneliness.

A noticeable characteristic of a nonplan family is that nobody's home. You can call there day or night and never get an answer! Everyone is continually rushing here and there, and with all the coming and going the home simply becomes a local motel and fast-food restaurant stop. It's because those living there have discovered that relationships are avoided, not developed, because those living there have discovered that relationships are too painful.

There is a process by which a person learns to avoid relationships:

As a child I realize that people:

get impatient with me,	reject me,
blame me,	hurt me,
yell at me,	deceive me.
lecture me	punish me
won't listen to me	

A door slams shut inside me. My inner voice says:

love hurts	I don't need
I can't trust love or big	your love
people	I won't ask for
	love

I erect barriers:

I am afraid	I become
I am inferior	aggressive
I become critical	and hostile
	I withdraw

I search for people to meet my needs:

business colleagues	a husband/
special acquaintances	wife
special interest groups	a close friend
	a substitute
	parent

If people fail me, I seek substitutes:

physical appearance	intelligence
sex appeal	degrees
security	titles
money	abilities
achievement	recognition
honors	

Loneliness Reproduces Itself

Loneliness reproduces loneliness within the family unit. We learn how to develop or destroy relationships through our primary models—parents! Growing up today, kids not only feel that their parents are too involved in their own changes to bother with their problems, but they also feel that the adult world offers them no models they would like to imitate, that being an adult means only more of the same—more insecurity, more instability, more unhappiness.[6]

The challenge is overwhelming! Raising children has never been more costly in terms of both time and money, and interference from the outside has never been more acute. Schools, peer pressure, television, and even "family experts" have invaded the home, robbing parents of much of their power without easing much of their responsibility. "Parents are not abdicating," says MIT psychologist Keniston: "They are being dethroned by forces they cannot influence, much less control." The pressure is intense! "We're the ultimate nuclear family, and sometimes I feel as if someone is trying to split the atom," says Georgia Houser, 35, a Houston college administrator and mother of three. And on occasion, a parent's plight can be sadly ludicrous: a 24-year-old drifter in Colorado sued his parents for $350,000, charging that their failure had made him what he is.[7]

Loneliness terrorism fills the family with heartache because everyone loses. The child loses a secure base from which to step out into the world; the parents, for all practical purposes, lose their child; and the husband and wife lose each other as they try to find themselves.

Loneliness, the terrorist, sucks the very life-force out of the family. Everyone is either frantically running from loneliness or running around trying to ease its pain. It's like a living death—people are dying emotionally, and therefore their most "intimate" relationships are dying as well.

4

The Pain Can Kill You!

Listen in on this diary from a suicide attempt that fortunately failed:

It is almost as if a fog of depressive and distorted feelings arrive to surround and suffocate me. I am aware at the time of my surrender, yet my reactions seem almost automatic, and with the passage of time and frequency of attacks, my efforts to resist become less and less powerful. The potpourri of feelings I experience are diverse yet have a familiar pattern and excruciating sting. It is almost as if a tape is staying within my head which triggers a wave of destructive thoughts and responses.

When I am in the midst of depression, I am very clear that I am in *BATTLE*. One side of me is yearning to live, share and relate to others (love)—yet another side feels powerless to ever bring these things about. It is from this feeling of not being able to change things that a pervasive sense of hopelessness feeds. During these times I feel as though I am not a part of the human race—a NON PERSON who doesn't fit into the scheme of things.

What angers me is that I view this non-acceptance as somehow sinful on my part—something for which I should be punished. It is as though there is an unloved, misfit side that is trying to annihilate the other side—which is child-like, spontaneous, good and loved. The cycle is a self-perpetuating one—the more isolated and alienated I feel the harder it is to integrate . . . . Yet the longer I am alone the more immobilized and debilitated I become. When I look beneath this collection of feelings what I really see is that I am not able to bear the pain of not connecting with others, of not sharing—in essence, of not loving. The hurt and desperate sense of LONELINESS are so excruciating and exhausting that during such times it simply seems logical to end the suffering—*to continue on seems like the crazy choice.*

How to Commit Suicide

Loneliness is an unhappy combination of

anxiety and insecurity, fear of rejection and failure, and a deep sense of loss and isolation—all feeding on the worry that the victim is both generally and specifically unloved and unwanted, by himself and others.[1]

In light of the vast amount of people in pain and the "logic" of the choice to commit suicide, now the ultimate how-to book is available: *A Guide to Self-Deliverance*. This 10,000-word British manual explains clearly and matter-of-factly how to commit suicide. This controversial book is published by Exit, a 6000-member British organization dedicated to "the right to die with dignity." According to Exit's general secretary, Nichols Reed, this book is a response to public demand. After the project was announced last fall, Exit's membership tripled in requests for the suicide manual.

Suicide in Slow Motion

Our society, suffocated with loneliness and failure, is more concerned with relief of pain and suffering than at any previous time. One-quarter of all medical prescriptions are for tranquilizers or pain-relieving drugs. More than half of the people who see physicians do so for non-specific complaints rather than for definite physical ailments. Our newspapers are full of advertisements urging lonely people, who may be despondent with the pain of loneliness, to call the Help Line or the Hot Line. If you cannot find love, you can call a dating service and a computer will match you to another lonely person. If your loneliness and irresponsibility fall into one of several common patterns, you may join an old, established group such as Alcoholics Anonymous or a new group such as Recovery Incorporated, Gamblers Anonymous, or Neurotics Anonymous. All of these groups bring lonely people together to relieve their suffering caused through loneliness and failure by getting them to help one another become more responsible through mutual involvement.

The need for involvement has been built into our nervous systems, and we always feel pain when we have no involvement. The pain warns us to seek involvement with others. If we fail in the attempt, there is always one possibility left for involvement: *ourselves*. Unsatisfactory and painful as this is in comparison with involvement with others who are worthwhile, involvement with ourselves will reduce and sometimes eliminate temporarily the pain of being alone. But because we need involvement with others, self-involvement is an inadequate alternative; we cannot fool our nervous system for long. Quickly dissatisfied with our self-involvement, it again responds with pain and we respond with further self-deception in response to the pain.[2]

To avoid the fact that we are really involved with ourselves, we have learned to focus our attention on a creation outside ourselves. We create and then concentrate on an idea, such as obsessive fear of germs; a behavior, such as compulsive gambling; a physical symptom, such as a migraine headache; or an emotion, such as depression. We focus on these self-creations as if they were real and separate from us. Keeping overly clean, gambling, suffering with (and treating) a headache, or being depressed then becomes our problem in place of our true problem—loneliness. We have *chosen* to act as we do because we desperately hope that the symptom or the behavior will provide enough involvement to satisfy what we should get from others. Over thousands of years of loneliness we have developed numerous self-involved symptoms and behaviors to keep us company and to reduce the pain of loneliness.[3]

Most medical practice is based on relieving the pain. Today millions of people go to doctors in an attempt to relieve the pain of depression and its close relatives—a host of nagging, painful complaints such as fatigue, headache, intestinal upset, muscular aches, and loss of interest in sex. Many doctors, however, do not understand that depression and most other such symptoms and complaints are companions. Trained to get rid of pain, they respond to the complaints of lonely and failing people by prescribing drugs that treat the aching symptom and not the true source of the problem—loneliness. It's placing a Band-Aid on a hemorrhage.[4]

All symptoms, whether psychological or psychosomatic, and all hostile, aggressive, irrational behavior are products of loneliness. These symptoms are companions to the lonely, failing, suffering people who struggle for an identity but do not succeed. Instead, they identify themselves as failures. The failure is focused onto a companion symptom to reduce the pain of loneliness. When the companion symptom itself is painful, a further attempt is made to reduce the pain with drugs and alcohol. Lonely people are running themselves into the ground—it's *suicide in slow motion!*[5]

Premature Death: Caused by Loneliness

Many clinicians sense that there is a relationship between loneliness, illness, and even premature death. Few cardiologists would deny that companionships and love may significantly prolong a patient's life. Yet in many urban hospital coronary care units, as many as 50 percent of discharged patients return to environments where they live alone.[6] The fact is that social isolation, the lack of human companionship, death, the absence of parents in early childhood, the sudden loss of love, and chronic human loneliness are significant contributors to premature death.[7]

Since we all must die, it is clear that neither human companionship or love can sustain life indefinitely. The question, then, is not whether human companionship or love can prevent cardiac disease. Rather, the question is whether the lack of human companionship and love, the sudden loss of human love, or the persistence of loneliness will lead to *premature* cardiac disease or excessive rates of disease and death. Does human companionship help sustain life? Does the lack of companionship hasten death? In addition to coronary heart disease, deaths attributed to hypertensive disease, cerebrovascular disease, rheumatic fever, chronic rheumatic heart disease, and cardiovascular disease all show the same pattern. *At all ages, for both sexes, and for all races in the United States, the unmarried always have higher death rates, sometimes as much as five times higher than those of married individuals.*[8]

The link between stress—more specifically loneliness—and the onset of illness is rapidly becoming a recognizable fact. Drs. James Lynch and William Convey at the University of Maryland have conducted significant studies concerning loneliness and its effects. They say that the evidence linking loneliness, or a sense of separateness, to disease and premature death appears consistently in population statistics, individual clinical histories, and even such famous prospective research as the Framingham Heart Study (when carefully scrutinized).

Although marital status is not clearly indicative of the presence or absence of the lonely state, a few comparative statistics in the premature death rates of white males in the United States reveal strikingly higher death rates in the unmarried. The reason for the increased mortality for many of the listed causes of death is quite clear: Statistics on deaths from suicide, automobile accidents, cirrhosis of the liver, and lung cancer are all significantly influenced by self-destructive human behavior. Yet similar increases in death rates appear in those major diseases that seem to be less obviously influenced by such behavior, such as stroke, heart disease, and cancer of the digestive system. We propose that the common source here is emotional upheaval and the sense of separateness, which then results in "dis-ease" and premature death at two different levels—behavior changes and physical changes—which can lead directly to premature death.[9]

Obviously, many people who are listed on mortality tables as married have lived in complete psychological and physical isolation, while the lives of many singles, widowed, and divorced individuals were filled with love. Yet even with this balanced understanding, it is phenomenal to observe the statistics that leap out on the mortality tables.

TABLE A

Marital Status and Mortality: Males

Cause of Death	Death Rates for White Men				Death Rates for Nonwhite Men			
	Married	Single	Widowed	Divorced	Married	Single	Widowed	Divorced
Coronary disease and other myocardial (heart) degeneration	176	237	275	362	142	231	328	298
Motor vehicle accidents	35	54	142	128	43	62	103	81
Cancer of respiratory system	28	32	43	65	29	44	56	75
Cancer of digestive organs	27	38	39	48	42	62	90	88
Vascular lesions (stroke)	24	42	46	58	73	105	176	132
Suicide	17	32	92	73	10	16	41	21
Cancer of lymph glands and of blood-making tissues	12	13	11	16	11	13	15	18
Cirrhosis of liver	11	31	48	79	12	40	39	53
Rheumatic fever (heart)	10	14	21	19	8	14	16	19
Hypertensive heart disease	8	16	16	20	49	68	106	90
Pneumonia	6	31	25	44	22	68	78	69
Diabetes mellitus	6	13	12	17	11	18	22	22
Homicide	4	7	16	30	51	79	152	129
Chronic nephritis (kidney)	4	7	7	7	11	18	23	21
Accidental falls	4	12	11	23	7	19	23	19
Tuberculosis, all forms	3	17	18	30	15	50	62	54
Cancer of prostate gland	3	3	3	4	8	7	15	12
Accidental fire or explosion	2	6	18	16	5	15	24	16
Syphilis	1	2	2	4	6	10	14	15

SOURCE: Hugh Carter and Paul C. Glick, *Marriage and Divorce: A Social and Economic Study*, American Public Health Association, Vital and Health Statistics Monograph (Cambridge: Harvard University Press, 1970), p. 345.

TABLE B

Marital Status and Mortality: Females

Cause of Death	Death Rates for White Women				Death Rates for Nonwhite Women			
	Married	Single	Widowed	Divorced	Married	Single	Widowed	Divorced
Coronary disease and other myocardial (heart) degeneration	44	51	67	62	83	112	165	113
Cancer of breast	21	29	21	23	19	26	28	27
Cancer of digestive organs	20	24	24	23	25	33	41	35
Vascular lesions (stroke)	19	23	31	28	72	89	147	82
Motor vehicle accidents	11	11	47	35	10	13	25	20
Rheumatic fever (heart)	10	14	15	13	8	14	12	13
Cancer of lymph glands and of blood-making tissues	8	9	9	8	7	9	9	13
Hypertensive heart disease	7	8	10	9	50	63	97	56
Cancer of cervix	7	4	13	18	17	22	34	27
Diabetes mellitus	7	7	11	8	20	24	36	22
Cirrhosis of liver	7	6	15	20	9	20	23	20
Cancer of ovary	7	12	8	8	6	8	9	8
Suicide	6	8	12	21	3	3	6	5
Cancer of respiratory system	5	5	6	7	5	6	6	10
Pneumonia	4	15	7	10	12	31	33	22
Chronic nephritis (kidney)	3	4	5	4	11	14	16	11
Homicide	2	1	7	9	14	17	33	25
Tuberculosis, all forms	2	5	4	5	8	24	19	16
Accidental fire or explosion	1	2	6	4	4	6	11	5

SOURCE: Hugh Carter and Paul C. Glick, *Marriage and Divorce: A Social and Economic Study*, American Public Health Association, Vital and Health Statistics Monograph (Cambridge: Harvard University Press, 1970), p. 345.

TABLE C

Marital Status and Cancer Death Ratios, 1960

Color and Primary Sites	Male Death Ratios			Female Death Ratios		
	Single to Married	Widowed to Married	Divorced to Married	Single to Married	Widowed to Married	Divorced to Married
WHITE						
Buccal cavity and pharynx	2.16*	2.12	4.10	0.87	1.47	1.67
Digestive organs and peritoneum	1.26	1.31	1.53	1.14	1.18	1.15
Respiratory system	1.16	1.45	2.11	1.04	1.23	1.49
Breast	2.50	2.50	2.50	1.41	1.02	1.13
Cervix uteri	—	—	—	0.60	1.66	2.38
Female genital organs excluding cervix	—	—	—	1.47	1.22	1.24
Prostate	0.90	1.13	1.30	—	—	—
Male genital organs except prostate	1.50	0.64	1.79	—	—	—
All urinary organs	1.10	1.28	1.52	1.08	1.25	1.40
Other and unspecified sites	1.26	1.33	1.70	1.17	1.29	1.22
Lymphatic and hematopoietic tissues	0.98	0.96	1.21	1.08	1.10	1.05
NONWHITE						
Buccal cavity and pharynx	2.08	2.64	3.14	1.50	1.94	1.44
Digestive organs and peritoneum	1.35	1.76	1.78	1.21	1.57	1.42
Respiratory system	1.51	1.74	2.46	1.23	1.63	1.89
Breast	1.67	3.33	2.00	1.31	1.41	1.42
Cervix uteri	—	—	—	1.17	1.84	1.60
Female genital organs excluding cervix	—	—	—	1.44	1.54	1.45
Prostate	0.88	1.52	1.45	—	—	—
Male genital organs except prostate	1.77	1.54	2.69	—	—	—
All urinary organs	1.17	2.16	1.83	1.13	1.68	1.70
Other and unspecified sites	1.34	1.87	1.95	1.31	1.49	1.37
Lymphatic and hematopoietic tissues	1.06	1.34	1.65	1.12	1.32	1.71

*2.16 means that the death rate for single white males for buccal cavity and pharynx cancer was 2.16 times higher than for married individuals. The married ratio would be 1.00 in all cases be 1.00.

SOURCE: Abraham M. Lilienfeld, Morton L. Levin and Irving I. Kessler, *Cancer in The United States.* Harvard University Press, Cambridge, Massachusetts, p. 126.

TABLE D
Marital Status and Rates of Institutionalization, 1960

Type of Institution	Married	Widowed	Divorced	Separated	Single
MEN					
In all institutions	45	340	676	589	935
Mental hospitals	22	97	237	215	550
State and local	18	76	183	189	472
Federal	3	16	48	23	72
Private	1	5	6	3	7
Correctional institutions	12	84	215	186	103
Homes for aged and needy:					
Known to have nursing care	1	38	29	30	40
Not known to have such care	3	68	103	64	91
Tuberculosis hospitals	6	35	62	63	36
Chronic hospitals (except tuberculosis and mental)	1	16	26	27	24
Institutions (mostly) for juveniles	0	2	4	4	89
WOMEN					
In all institutions	37	99	193	247	475
Mental hospitals	31	51	150	193	297
State and local	30	48	144	187	286
Federal	1	1	3	5	4
Private	1	2	3	2	7
Correctional institutions	1	2	5	9	2
Homes for aged and needy:					
Known to have nursing care—	1	16	10	10	26
Not known to have such care—	1	21	17	12	38
Tuberculosis hospitals	2	4	5	10	6
Chronic hospitals (except tuberculosis and mental)	1	4	4	9	8
Institutions (mostly) for juveniles	0	1	2	4	97

SOURCE: Carter and Glick, *Marriage and Divorce*, p. 334.
*Slight mathematical discrepancies were unexplained in original source

In what remains one of the most comprehensive retrospective studies of early predictors of disease and premature death, Drs. Ralph Paffenbarger and his colleagues examined the records of up to 50,000 former students from Harvard University and the University of Pennsylvania who were in college during the

TABLE E
*Coronary Heart Disease Death Rates per 100,000 Population, 1959-1961**

Color, sex, and marital status	25-34	35-44	45-54	55-64	65-74	75-84	85+
White Males							
Married	9.6	81.1	329.6	849.3	1,836.2	3,735.6	7,798.7
Single	14.6	119.0	458.4	1,086.7	2,512.8	5,053.7	9,913.3
Widowed	19.0	149.0	548.3	1,314.2	2,662.6	5,184.5	10,504.1
Divorced	27.2	200.0	713.3	1,634.3	3,070.8	5,815.5	10,719.6
White Females							
Married	1.8	11.8	60.1	254.4	864.2	2,401.0	5,374.4
Single	5.7	24.6	80.2	262.6	906.2	3,022.3	8,749.8
Widowed	9.3	27.6	101.7	376.1	1,162.9	3,243.8	8,398.7
Divorced	4.1	25.3	95.9	331.1	1,038.2	3.177.1	7,522.3
Nonwhite Males							
Married	14.7	77.7	257.2	643.1	1,246.1	1,999.8	3,698.9
Single	33.0	158.5	456.4	857.8	1,822.9	3,096.2	5,259.1
Widowed	62.3	202.6	682.6	1,442.6	2,285.6	3,175.0	5,850.4
Divorced	38.8	188.3	595.5	1,226.2	2,229.7	2,977.7	6,386.7
Nonwhite Females							
Married	9.7	41.4	147.8	371.3	677.5	1,337.1	2,312.2
Single	15.6	75.8	205.3	426.0	951.8	1,856.4	4,417.4
Widowed	23.0	100.2	318.4	772.8	1,264.8	2,083.7	4,420.7
Divorced	12.2	55.8	207.6	517.7	943.4	1,783.8	2,990.3

*Note that these are death *rates*, not comparable ratios of nonmarried to married people. In every case, the death rates for married people are lower.

period from 1921 through 1950. They carefully examined the college records of the first 590 male students who had died of coronary heart disease and contrasted them with 1180 randomly chosen classmates of equivalent age who were known to be alive. Nine factors distinguished the coronary heart disease victims: heavy cigarette smoking, higher levels of blood pressure, increased body weight, shortness of body height, *early parental death, absence of siblings, nonparticipation in sports* (coupled with a general college style of *secretiveness* and *social isolation*), a higher emotional index, and scarlet fever in childhood.[10]

Dr. J.J. Groen at the University of Leiden has

also linked marital status and the lack of love to the development of coronary heart disease. He observed: "It appears that the individuals who are supported by love and secure family and community bonds can cope much better with stressful psychological situations than individuals who are deprived of such support."[11]

She Died of a Broken Heart

Growing numbers of people now accept the idea that emotional stress might predispose them to develop heart problems. Yet at the same time, far fewer people seem ready to accept the possibility that the lack of human companionship could do the same thing. In the context of human disease, stress and anxiety are now generally accepted as bad for one's health, while human companionship is still generally viewed as irrelevant. But it's not![12]

Loneliness (lack of companionship) is a killer, whether by pressuring a suicide attempt, cultivating psychological problems, or intensifying the possibility of disease. But there is another way that loneliness kills—*the pain can kill you!* It's the pain of a broken heart! It *is* possible to die of a broken heart, and hearts may break when all *former* sources of attention and love are gone.[13]

I had the privilege of knowing a very beautiful lady whose name was Hilda. Hilda was a healthy and complete person in every way. She was devoted to being a wife and mother. She had a large family-support system of six brothers and sisters with their families, all living within a 35-mile radius. Every "exceptional" adjective was used to describe her by her family and friends.

One by one Hilda began losing her support system. Her mother died, then her sister, then her father, and finally her intimate support— her husband. The stress and pain of her great loneliness took its toll. It was discovered that she was eaten up with bone cancer with less than a year to live. I watched her die slowly throughout the next ten months. All the time I thought she was dying of cancer. Now I know better. Cancer was the ultimate blow that killed her, but in reality *she died of a broken heart*.

Hilda was my mother.

I know now that the pain of loneliness can kill.

5

I'm Not O.K.,
You're Not O.K.,
and That's O.K.!

*It is becoming more and more obvious
that it is not starvation, not microbes,
not cancer, but man himself who is
mankind's greatest danger.*—Carl Jung

The future, the people, and the self seem out
of control! However, the primary problem
doesn't rest in the future or in our relationships
with other people, but in how man views
himself as he faces the future and relates to people. The problem most critical to mankind and
his loneliness is the *nature of man*.

As man comes face to face with himself,
even the predictions of the optimists tend to
carry promotions of disaster; Teilhard de
Chardin, for all his buoyancy, wrote in
December 1953, 2½ years before his death,
"Man now sees that the seeds of his ultimate
dissolution are at the heart of his being. The
End of the Species is in the marrow, is in our
bones!" Norman O. Brown, descending
momentarily from his rarefied romanticism,

wrote, "Today even the survival of humanity is a utopian hope."

Why are even the optimists so gloomy when it comes to declaring the future of man? Why is it that we know so much and yet fail so miserably in human communications and relationships? Why is it that we have so much material on self-help and success and yet feel like we must have more help and resign ourselves to failure? Why do people insist on telling us that man is basically good, when we have experienced more wars in this century than in all the other centuries put together? Why is it that even though I'm told "I'm O.K." and "You're O.K.," I don't really buy it in my gut?

The answer to these questions is: *Man is basically not O.K.!* I'm not O.K. and you're not O.K. If we can understand this as the "bottom line" of human nature, then that's O.K.

Alienation Is Not O.K.

To understand the nature of man we must be willing to look at his wounds and frailties. It would be more pleasant to pretend that everything is just sailing along, but the casualties in human society must be counted. Reaching for Band-Aids to cover the gashes is looking for patchwork remedies to specific problems. It is necessary to ask why man bleeds—why I'm not O.K. and you're not O.K. We seem to be waging all-out wars against the symptoms, the fevers, and the aches of man, but war against symptoms is futile. If man feels some suggestions of his own divinity, he is also painfully aware that the forces he has created have cast deep shadows across his throne. Man, the self-proclaimed lord of the universe, can and does feel very lost. The ambivalence of his emotions is uncomfortable, vacillating between the distant hope that human ingenuity will someday solve our problems and the despair of living with those problems.

Human nature abhors a vacuum. And in this moment the ache of emptiness (loneliness) inside man is obvious in the shocking statistics on our national mental health. Two-thirds of all the hospital beds being occupied at this moment in the United States are occupied by mental patients. More than one out of every ten Americans has already undergone some form of psychotherapy. More than one out of every ten college students is established to be so emotionally crippled that it will be impossible for him to finish his education.[1]

Man is quickly becoming alienated from his world. Science is predicting controlled weather, controlled population, and even controlled human behavior, but man seems hopelessly lost and out of control. The world that seems to be moving more and more into man's hands also seems to be stepping away from him. He is something like a domineering parent, who simultaneously loves to control and yet loses communication with his child.

It's like the modern astronaut who goes out to explore outer space but is scientifically and hygenically protected from any real contact with it. Alienation from environment, people, and self is the guts of loneliness.[2]

Man feels powerless to cope with life as it is. If a person is afflicted with a sense of his own impotence and insignificance, self-alienation and self-hatred cannot be far away. The self-estranged person is not only a stranger to himself but is also an alien to his world, and this is the soil in which self-hatred flourishes. Man learns to despise not only his uselessness and insignificance but also his very self. And from self-hatred there is a second, almost-automatic step to the hatred of others, and especially of the institutions and the establishment that have made man feel so small. Man is like a basin; when he fills up with anything, that with which he is filled is bound to run over the sides and spill out onto others.[3]

Alienation is not O.K.

Depersonalization Is Not O.K.

In addition to the problem of alienation is another element that belongs in the loneliness package—the problem of depersonalization: Loneliness breeds the feeling of being a *nonperson!*

A variety of voices are effectively chipping away at man's personness. One voice says that man is nothing but a collection of molecules. This view reduces man to the explanation of his parts. But where is "man" in this collection of molecules? Another voice says that man is nothing but a machine. Man is only the product of his environment. He is just a stimulus-response machine with all its nonpersonality. Still another voice says that man is nothing but an animal. Here man is depersonalized to an impersonal biological organism.

Man cannot live within these impersonal systems for one very simple reason—his own personness! Personal man just doesn't fit within the impersonal! It's like a fish attempting to live out of water, or a train maneuvering through a field without a set of tracks. It just doesn't fit. The result? Intense loneliness. That's not O.K.

Fear Is Not O.K.

The loneliness package is filled with alienation and depersonalization, but inside the core of loneliness is fear. Fear paralyzes a person at every level of life.

There are three primary fears at the core of loneliness. The first is the *fear of identity with the accompanying pain of dissatisfaction.* People just do not know who they are. So many communications are bombarding us that we are tied in knots of confusion. So much in the world is directing us that it is difficult to keep one's unique identity alive. People are trying to "find themselves," and yet they fear what they might discover. Along with the fear of identity is a great pain of dissatisfaction. It seems that nothing is available that truly satisfies.

Christopher Lasch in *The Culture of Narcissism* described this dissatisfaction: "In the last twenty-five years, the borderline patient, who confronts the psychiatrist not with well-defined symptoms but with diffuse dissatisfactions, has become increasingly common. He does not suffer from debilitating fixations or phobias or from the conversion of repressed sexual energy into nervous ailments; instead he complains of vague, diffuse dissatisfactions with life and feels his amorphous existence to be futile and purposeless. He describes subtly experienced yet pervasive feelings of emptiness and depression, violent oscillations of self-esteem only by attaching himself to strong, admired figures whose acceptance he craves and by whom he needs to feel supported. Although he carries out his daily responsibilities and even achieves distinction, happiness eludes him, and life frequently strikes him as not worth living."[4]

The fear of identity with its pain of dissatisfaction positions people in a "perpetual state of unsatisfied desire." Seemingly, no matter what you try to stuff into that inner vacuum of dissatisfaction, nothing fits quite right! That is loneliness!

The second fear is the *fear of inadequacy with*

the accompanying pain of depreciation. It is a sense of inadequacy as a person. The person who feels deeply inferior (as we all do to some extent) may be aware of certain particular abilities, but there is inside him the gnawing parasite of his own inadequacy. He feels that he has very little personal worth.[5] It's a fear of inadequacy—worthlessness! Its companion pain is the feeling of depreciation (out of date, out of sync), like an old car that has lost its value and is falling apart. It's a feeling that no one would help us if we were in trouble, that what happens to us, whether good or bad, makes no difference to the world around us—that we ourselves make no difference.[6]

In a sense, the third fear is the most inner fear of the three. It is the *fear of intimacy with the accompanying pain of detachment.* The fears of identity and inadequacy are merely spin-offs of the universal fear of intimacy.

The fear of intimacy is derived from frequent failures in communication. The combination of failures in the areas of social and conversational skills, nonverbal communication, and response to feedback is a powerful one, capable of completely screening off a person and insulating him from any hope of contact with people, whether generally or intimately. The combination is sadly effective in another way as well, since it not only reflects but also contributes to those psychological states that are most symbolic and symptomatic of the condition of loneliness. Probably the best-known and most easily recognized of these psychological states are depression and anxiety, insecurity and inadequacy, shyness and lack of a well-defined, realistic self-image.[7]

Loneliness is caused not by being alone but by being without some definite needed relationship or set of relationships. Loneliness appears always to be a response to the absence of some particular type of relationship or, more accurately, a response to the absence of some particular relational provision. In many instances it is a response to the absence of the provisions of an intimate attachment.[8] A substantial proportion of all the lonely people feel themselves to be without much love for themselves or anyone else. This is due not so much to a shortage in the supply of love and affection as to failures in the channels of communication.[9]

We can define loneliness as a feeling of deprivation or detachment caused by the lack of certain kinds of human contact: the feeling that someone is missing. And since one has to have had some expectation of what it was that would be in this empty space, loneliness can further be characterized as the sense of detachment that comes when certain *expected* human relationships are absent.[10]

Another experience essential to man's fulfillment of himself involves the group—that is, three or more persons who come into meaningful interpersonal relationships. The group contributes to self-fulfillment in a way that cannot be achieved by the person alone or in person-to-person meetings.[11] All loneliness syndromes seem to give rise to yearning for the relationship—an intimacy, a friendship, a relationship with kin—that would provide whatever is at the moment insufficient.[12]

The desperate search for a relationship to fill the void of detachment is the motivating factor behind the family breakdown. Everyone is desperate for intimacy, but the price of becoming vulnerable is too painful to pursue.

Self-defeating solutions are everywhere! Arising out of a pervasive dissatisfaction with the quality of personal relationships, people are advised not to make too large an investment or commitment in love and friendship, to avoid excessive dependence on others, and to live for the moment—the very conditions that created the crisis of loneliness in the first place.[13]

Pain Is Not O.K.

In the final analysis loneliness is the fear of pain—the pain of dissatisfaction, depreciation, and detachment. As we try to reduce the pain of loneliness we may suffer depression, jealousy, suspicion, greed, revenge, hate, guilt, shame, and boredom. Although all of these feelings are painful, none is as painful as becoming directly aware that we are alone, rejecting and rejected by others around us. If we are unable to substitute any of these common feelings for the pain of loneliness and if we remain detached, our nervous system may become so overwhelmed with the pain of loneliness that we choose to escape into unreality.[14]

As the bumper sticker says: "Reality is only for those who can't cope with drugs." In the everyday lives of many lonely people the pain is constant and gnawing. Discouraged because they do not believe they can get involved, many respond to the urge to escape the pain by taking what seems to them the best choice available for relief from the nagging ache. More than 20 million people in the country use alcohol or drugs regularly, both of which do relieve the pain—until the effect wears off.[15]

In avoiding the pain of loneliness everyone seems to be looking for fast, temporary relief of pain. It really doesn't make any difference what is used as the pain killer as long as it relieves the pain for now. It may be "self-awareness," "positive thinking," "success motivation," "holistic" lifestyle, EST, Lifespring, TA, TM, or maybe even pseudo-Christianity. Each of these is used as an aspirin, a high, a trip, or an anesthetic for the fast, temporary relief of pain.

Why We're Not O.K.

Why is man not O.K.? Why do we all experience alienation, depersonalization, fear, and pain? If the cause were purely environmental, then some people would experience these problems and others would not. But it's not an external, environmental problem. The cause is internal. Man is basically not O.K.! Man is not O.K. because he is not normal in his present state. He is abnormal!

For me, the most reasonable explanation for man's abnormal state is in the Bible. Man was created perfect and complete. He was normal in his original state. But through his rebellion against his Creator, man became abnormal. In his normal condition "man and his wife were both naked and not ashamed." They had total communication and intimacy, free from inhibitions. After man's rebellion he hid himself from his Creator and his mate. He felt alienation, depersonalization, fear, and pain for the first time. He realized that he was definitely not O.K.!

If man today were normal by not being O.K., then there would not be much hope of man getting any better. However, since man's state is *abnormal* today, there is hope for positive change—to move back toward normality. So man was once O.K., now is not O.K., and has the hope of being O.K. in the future! I'M NOT O.K., YOU'RE NOT O.K., and that's O.K. because there is hope!

PART TWO

Love: A Taste of Heaven!

6

Loneliness Is a Decision

Poor Johnson had spent his life making wrong decisions. If he bet on a horse, it would lose; if he chose one elevator rather than another, it would stall between floors; the line he picked before the bank teller's cage never moved; the lane he chose in traffic crawled; the day he picked for a picnic produced a cloudburst; and so it went, day after day, year after year.

Then it became necessary for Johnson to travel to some city a thousand miles away, and to do it quickly. A plane was the only possible conveyance that would get him there in time, and it turned out that only one company supplied only one flight that would do. His heart bounded. There was no choice to make; and if he made no choice, surely he would come to no grief!

He took the plane.

Imagine his horror when, midway in the flight, the plane's engines caught fire and it became obvious that the plane would crash in moments.

Johnson broke into fervent prayer to his favorite saint, Saint Francis. He pleaded, "I have never in my life made the right choice. Why this should be I don't know, but I have borne my cross and have not complained. On this occasion, however, I did not make a choice; this was the only plane I could take, and I had to take it. Why, then, am I being punished?"

He had no sooner finished when a giant hand swooped down out of the clouds and somehow snatched him from the plane. There he was, miraculously suspended two miles above the earth's surface, while the plane spiraled downward far below.

A heavenly voice came down from the clouds. "My son, I can save you if you have in truth called upon me."

"Yes, I called on you," cried Johnson. "I called on you, Saint Francis!"

"Ah," said the heavenly voice; "Saint Francis Xavier or Saint Francis of Assisi? Which?"

Decisions! Choices! Commitments! Life is a

series of responsibilities (which demand decisions, choices, and commitments) lived out in the context of relationships. Every day we are faced with choices. At the same time we have become experts at avoiding those choices and responsibilities.

Some people are very decisive, but only when it comes to avoiding decisions.

Avoiding decisions has precipitated the problem of irresponsibility at all levels of society. The mood of the day is to blame everybody and everything for what is wrong, but by all means not to accept personal responsibility for making the right or wrong decisions. This is where we get things like "guilty by reason of insanity" (not really guilty) or "the Devil made me do it" (I didn't really do it). It is said that when the boss is smiling during a crisis, he has found someone or something to blame the problem on!

Germs and Disease: "Out There"

Until the late nineteenth century, most people did not believe that they were responsible for their own physical health, a belief that has lingered on into the late twentieth century. Even today, many people resist the idea that there is a connection between their loneliness and their health. They will believe that human disease is caused by germs "out there" and that nothing they do matters.[1]

Psychologically, the exact same avoidance is

used. People find much comfort in labeling their problems "allergies" or "diseases" or in blaming their parents and life circumstances. Even for some Christians, instead of personal responsibility the "spiritual" thing is to be "led by God." The incredible thing is that God seems to "lead" people to do the strangest, most unethical, irresponsible things! That which is responsible is always outside ourselves—"out there."

Psychosis (mental disorientation—acting crazy) is rarely understood as a choice by either the adult who adopts it or by the people who are involved with him: his doctor, family, employer, or friends. If anyone involved with him suspects that the psychosis is indeed a choice, he finds it difficult to say so. Voicing such a suspicion makes everyone uncomfortable because everyone then has, or might believe he has, some responsibility for not relieving the loneliness that caused the patient to choose psychosis. It is much easier for everyone to believe that the person just "got sick" and that no one has any responsibility for what happened.

In addition, we do not like to admit that craziness is a choice, because we are all a little crazy at times; if we admit that it is a choice for others, we must also admit that it is a choice for ourselves. The patient will not admit that he had made a choice because he would then see that both his previous lonely life and his present crazy life are self-created. His symptoms are of course specifically chosen to help him avoid such an understanding. The doctor will not admit that it is a choice because he would then have to admit that mental illness as a disease is only a scientific fantasy. Such an admission would conflict with his omnipotent healing role—a doctor cannot heal craziness as he can appendicitis or streptococcus sore throat.[2]

Traditional counseling avoids action in the present by delving into the past to discover when the patient first experienced failure and loneliness. It is important to understand why you feel the way you feel and how past experiences have affected you. But much of the time a search into the past is harmful because it almost always becomes an end in itself, an intellectual involvement that precludes the lonely person from doing now what he should be doing in the real world: *learning to become successfully involved with others.*

It is wrong to avoid the issue of present behavior by searching for remote periods of loneliness or for rejections early in life, when the symptom was learned. The wrong is compounded by excusing a patient's lonely, incompetent involvement with his symptom by labeling the symptom an illness. Three errors—encouraging the patient to blot out the present, excusing the patient's involvement with the symptom, and labeling his symptom an illness—relieve the patient from the responsibility of learning successful involvement with others, of facing his loneliness and failure, and of admitting that his symptom is his own choice.[3]

Life As a Ping-Pong Ball

The reason that many of us never even begin to break away from the grip of loneliness is that we insist on making others responsible for our individual fears of love and intimacy. This was natural when we were helpless, dependent little people. But in playing the role of victims beyond childhood it is possible to go through life merely *reacting* to other people and events, and never assuming personal responsibility for *acting*. *Where that is the case, loneliness is of our own doing.*⁴ Victimizing ourselves into reactionaries is like volunteering to be a ping-pong ball—knocked around by anyone who wants to play!

The loneliest people are those who have decided to stop loving. It's a choice! It is of our own doing. We may sometimes say that we gave good reasons for doing so. But whenever we do, it is because we have allowed ourselves to be hurt to the point that we actually believe "it's all their fault." *Victims always feel lonely.* As long as we keep justifying or defending our position, there is no hope of breaking free from the shackles of loneliness.⁵

As victims, therefore, we are unwilling to take responsibility for our *decisions, feelings*, and *behavior*. The prospect is frightening. We are forever mumbling, "If it weren't for them . . . you . . . her . . . him." But behind this theme song is a fear of accepting personal responsibility for our own decisions. We always turn sour. We are not willing to give a firm and resounding yes or no to anything or anyone. Characterized by such halfhearted statements as "I'll try," "maybe," "I suppose," and "I hope so," we do anything to avoid having to make a definite commitment.[6]

Hope Inside Loneliness

If loneliness were a disease savagely attacking human beings everywhere, then there would be little hope for a quick discovery of its cure. *But loneliness is not a disease. It's a decision!* It's a decision to avoid the fears of the pain accompanying *identity* (companion pain of dissatisfaction), *inadequacy* (companion pain of depreciation), and *intimacy* (companion pain of detachment). *Since loneliness is a decision and not a disease, there is hope!* If a decision or series of decisions made me lonely, then a decision or series of decisions can relieve my loneliness. Inside loneliness is hope.

From Loneliness to Love

Man is essentially alone and lonely, and from this isolation he cannot be saved by someone else but only by himself through the fact that he loves. *It is the fear of love which is the root cause of every attitude and form of behavior that separates us from each other.* The most telling sign of our personness—our fear—is difficult to detect, and sometimes even feel, because it is not always characterized by a sudden onset of trembling, sweating palms, or knots in the stomach. Since it is a root condition of life, it is an inherent component of our personhood.[7]

We are lonely because of our fear to love. The fear of love is the foundational fear which underlies the fear of identity (the love of who you are), the fear of inadequacy (the love of what you do), and the fear of intimacy (the love of others).

Loneliness and love go hand in hand. To be aware of love, in its real sense, is loneliness: the hopes, the joys, the ecstasy, the tensions of loss and fulfillment of dreams and despair—this awareness that love is now but is also passing (that one reaches out to hold the moment and suddenly it is gone, sealed in the past in mere memories), the knowledge that love can never exist again. Loneliness is an inevitable outcome of real love, but it is also a process through which new love becomes possible. Love has no meaning without loneliness; loneliness is the other side of love. *Just as people decide to be lonely, so there must be a decision to love!*[8]

Make an Appointment with Yourself

Our greatest mistake is in not distinguishing between "belong alone" and "loneliness." Our periods of being alone, if simply allowed to happen to be experienced by ourselves, can be among the most rewarding of our lives. It *is* possible to be alone and not be lonely.[9] But let's look again at Erich Fromm's comments about being alone: "We have developed a phobia of being alone; we prefer the utmost trivial and even obnoxious company, the most meaningless activities, to being alone with ourselves; we seem to be frightened at the prospect of facing ourselves. Is it because we feel we would be such bad company?" (Erich Fromm, *Man for Himself*). We need to face ourselves so desperately, but we fear it so much! At the innermost core of all loneliness is a deep and powerful yearning for union—an appointment—with one's lost self.

The saying "If you can't make it with people you can't make it" has a corollary: "If you can only make it with people, and not alone, you can't make it."[10] Being alone has a quality of immediacy and depth; it is a significant experience—one of the few in modern life in which man communes with himself. And in such communion man comes to grips with his own being. He discovers life: who he is, what he really wants, the meaning of his existence, the true nature of his relations with others. He may see and realize for the first time truths which have been obscured for a long time. Distortions suddenly become naked and transparent.[11]

It is in this state of naked isolation that the potential for growth and change exist. Being alone is an important place to make an appointment with yourself.

But if your experiences of being alone are not by appointment, but come from the flow of natural events, over which you have no control, there are two options: 1) by not allowing yourself to accept them the separation can defeat you and leave you in a state of unresolved despair for the rest of your life, deciding that you will never risk loving again; 2) allowing yourself to accept being alone can serve ultimately to bring out the best possibilities. It can give you the time to examine who you are and what you want, to evaluate your goals and the quality of your work, and to appreciate your husband, your wife, your friends, or even God.[12]

Loneliness is not a disease. It's a decision—a decision based upon the fear of love! A psychiatrist was asked, "How can you teach people to love?" He answered the question by one of his own: "Have you ever had a toothache?" He made his point. When we are in pain, even if it is only the passing discomfort of a toothache, we are thinking about ourselves.

The psychiatrist continued: "This is a pain-filled world in which we are living. And the pains that reside deep in the human hearts around us are not like toothaches. We go to bed at night with them and we wake up with them in the morning . . . . This is a painfilled world, and so a loveless world that we live in. Most human beings are so turned-in by their own pains that they cannot get enough out of themselves to love to any great extent."[13]

Loneliness is a decision based upon the fear of love. *In order to counteract loneliness and all of its masquerades, another decision is necessary—a decision to love and be loved.*

A wealthy lady and her maid were discussing the maid's dating life. The lady asked, "Do you allow just any man to kiss you?" "No, I just allow those I know and those I love." The lady was shocked by her maid's answer and said, "But that's a lot of men. What's the difference between *those you know* and *those you love*? How do you decide?" The maid quickly responded, "Well, those I know, I let. And those I love, I help!"

A decision to love and be loved is critical in relieving loneliness. But a decision alone is not enough. Like the maid, you must decide and do something!

7

Pseudolove

It's a law of human life, as certain as gravity: *to live fully, we must learn to use things and love people—not love things and use people.*

Pseudolove is the term I use to describe the "man-love" that emerges from the fear of love itself. None of us wants to be a fraud or to live a lie; none of us wants to be a sham or a phony, but the fears that we experience and the risks that honest self-communication would involve seem so intense to us that seeking refuge in our roles, masks, and games become an almost-natural reflex action.[1]

Pseudolove: Fear of Love

It is well past midnight when Mike and Helen Brown put down their coffee cups and rise to leave the Schmidt's. As they stand by the doorway saying the reluctant goodbyes of a delightful evening, Helen feels a sudden rush of warmth and love. Her impulse is to throw her arms around Jane Schmidt and tell her how much their friendship means to her. But just as suddenly the impulse is somehow slightly stifled. Instead, she reaches out, touches Jane's arm lightly, and says, "It's been a wonderful evening!"

While she settles into the seat beside Mike as they drive away, she continues to bask in the glow of pleasure she has felt throughout the evening. "But it's strange," she thinks to herself with vague feelings of disappointment, "that I couldn't show Jane how much I care for her."

At about the same time in another part of the city, Mary Blake calls to her husband, "Jim, aren't you coming to bed now?" As he goes to the bedroom door and sees Mary already in bed, Jim senses the familiar desire rising within him. "Twelve years married and she's still beautiful," he thinks to himself. And at this moment she looks very inviting.

But Jim's urge to throw off his clothes and jump into bed passes quickly. Instead, he steps to the bed, kisses her tenderly, but without passion, and says, "I'm not really very sleepy yet, honey. I think I'll stay up and watch the late show."

Leaving the room, he half hopes that she will make her invitation unmistakably explicit, but she only says, "Good night, sweetheart!" and he settles before the television, thinking to himself, "Well, if I had gone ahead she might have turned away with an 'I think I'm just too tired tonight.' "

Mary, meanwhile, turns restlessly in bed for many minutes, filled with sexual desire and the longing to be caressed. She is more disappointed than angry or hurt. "Perhaps I could have told him I wanted him," she thinks to herself, but is surprised to notice a shiver of fear pass through her at the thought of expressing her desire so directly.

It is one of the more puzzling facets of human existence that we often avoid those experiences that we most desire. We long to give and receive expressions of love, but at the critical moment we frequently back away. Our avoidance of longed-for experiences is rooted in fear. We are afraid of freedom, afraid of sexual enjoyment, and afraid of being ourselves with other people. And the most basic of all these fears is our fear of emotional closeness with others. It's the fear of love, and that is what I call pseudolove.[2]

Growth in a Vacuum?

Harry Stack Sullivan, one of the more eminent psychiatrists of interpersonal relationships in our times, has propounded the theory that all personal growth, all personal damage and regression, and all personal healing and growth come through our relationship with others. There is a persistent suspicion in most of us that we can solve our own problems and be the masters of our own ships of life, but the fact of the matter is that by ourselves we can only be consumed by our problems and suffer shipwreck. *What I am, at any given moment in the process of my becoming a person, will be determined by my relationships with those who love me or refuse to love.*

A love relationship will be only as good as the communication. If two people can honestly tell each other what each thinks, judges, values, loves, honors, and also what each esteems, hates, fears, desires, hopes for, believes in, and is committed to, then and only then can each person grow. Then and only then can each person be what he really is, say what he really thinks, tell what he really feels, and express what he really loves.[3]

When true love is unable to emerge, and pseudolove reigns in your life and relationships, loneliness appears and is intensified! The true love which promotes personal growth cannot blossom in a vacuum but only in a relationship. You cannot find yourself by yourself, but only in relationship with someone else.

Most people vacillate back and forth between the two extremes of relationships—independence and dependence. It's an almost paradoxical relationship between independence and dependence. A desperate attempt to prove one's independence from significant relationships is coupled with a deep-rooted insecurity about relationships and a fear that he will be abandoned by those who are important to him. Without full awareness of what is happening, a person dedicates his life to the proposition that "half a loaf is better than none." In other words, he settles for a partial relationship rather than risk no relationship at all. Due to his insecurity he doesn't feel truly independent. Therefore he cannot risk letting others see his dependency that in reality is simply a new means of controlling the other person and seducing him into staying around.[4]

Pseudolove only understands the isolation of independence or the suffocation of dependence. It stands against the most critical dynamic of human relationships—*the principle of interdependence.* Pseudolove blocks and blurs every possible channel for the interdependence of true love to exist.

Block of Selfishness

The first blockage of true love's interdependence is the *block of selfishness.* As we saw earlier, the pain is so great in this painfilled world that there is a tremendous urge to turn inward to ourselves. This urge is primarily for survival. But selfishness creates a blockage that prevents true love and instead promotes loneliness! Therefore, survival is also destroyed in the process.

Selfishness is not identical with self-love but is actually its very opposite. Selfishness is one kind of greediness. Like all greediness, it contains an insatiability, as a consequence of which there is never any real satisfaction.

Greed is a bottomless pit which exhausts the person in an endless effort to satisfy the need without ever reaching satisfaction. The selfish person is always restless, always driven by the fear of not getting enough, of missing something, of being deprived of something. He is filled with burning envy of anyone who might have more. This type of person is basically not fond of himself at all, but deeply dislikes himself. Selfishness is rooted in this very lack of fondness for oneself. He loves neither others nor himself.[5]

Selfishness also says, "I love oranges!" That expression means "Oranges do something for me." And when I get through squeezing all I can out of an orange, then I discard that orange. Selfish people love people as they love oranges, and discard them in the same way.

Block of Treadmills

The second blockage of true love's interdependence is the *block of treadmills*. Pseudo-love places "loved ones" on a performance basis—a treadmill. It's a conditional sort of love that says, "I love you, if . . ." or "I love you, but . . .!"

The usual demands made by conditional (parental) love are: compliance, cooperation, conformity, being like somebody, doing one's best always, being a success, working hard, causing no trouble, glorifying the family name, making one's parents proud, etc. Naturally, under conditions like these one can only fail, and in failure be deprived of love. Failure means that you didn't pay the necessary price of admission to love. This leads to self-hatred, whether consciously admitted or not. *And this self-hatred is the beginning of a sad and self-destructive life of loneliness.*[6]

To be loved because of one's merit, because one deserves it, always leaves doubt; maybe I did not please the person whom I want to love me, maybe this or that—there is always a fear that love could disappear. Furthermore, "deserved" love tends to leave a bitter feeling that one is not loved for oneself, that one is loved only because one pleads, that in the last analysis one is not loved at all but is merely used.[7]

Block of Walls

The third blockage of true love's interdependence is the *block of walls.* These walls are built by all the debris, wreckage, and waste that have piled up in a relationship over a period of time. The piles of waste increase as people cover up their true feelings or smooth over conflicts in their relationship.

Again, the problem reverts back to the fear of pain—the fear of the pain involved in confrontation. The pain is so great that the cover-up is used to prevent potential confrontation and the smooth-over is used to repair the breakage of a confrontation in process. The fact of the matter is that you cannot be successful in preventing confrontation by the cover-up, nor can you repair the breakage of confrontation through smoothing things over! What you will accomplish is the pileup of waste that will continue to distance you from one another toward greater loneliness. Without some kind of plan to eliminate the walls of waste, interdependence will not be achieved and loneliness will not be relieved.

Blur of the Ideal Love

The first blur of true love's interdependence is the *blur of the ideal love.* Usually, when a man and a woman first "fall in love," it is not with the reality of the other person but with a projection of what a loved one should be. It may be that the projected image is derived from a mother or a father or a dream. Carl Jung says that "every man carried his Eve in himself," meaning that every man carries in his subconscious the image of what a lovable woman is. Likewise, every Eve carries her Adam within herself. This is why certain men "fall for" certain types of women, and vice versa. The ideal image may, in some cases, have very little relationship to the real person. The problem, of course, is that if the person insists on keeping the ideal image and making the other person conform to it, he will love only an image, only a projection. He will never get to know the other person.[8]

The most common arrangement in marriages is the blur of the ideal love. Many women end up marrying their "father" and become the "mischievous child" relating to his nagging, straight, rigid, disciplinary "mother." The woman moves into the little-girl role and relates to her husband as her "father," who must be manipulated and played up to. Neither man nor woman relates as lovers. Neither enters into interdependence. Neither discovers the relief that is effective in alleviating the pain of loneliness.

Blur of Ownership

The second blur of true love's interdependence is the *blur of ownership*. True love is not "to have and to hold," but the blur of ownership demands it. "To have" is to possess and "to hold" is to protect the one you love. But who in the final analysis is able to possess or protect anybody else?

The blur of ownership is being responsible *for* another person rather than being responsible *to* him or her. You cannot really be responsible *for* anybody but yourself. When you remain responsible *for* yourself and responsible *to* everyone else, you are influencing others to be responsible for themselves.

But when you are involved in the blur of

ownership, you run everybody's life but your own. Fortune-telling and mind-reading become a manner of communication. It happens like this: "If I had told you, you would have blown up!" "You don't care about me." "You always do this." "You never do that." When a person has already pegged you or placed you in a box, the motivation for communication vanishes. You feel taken for granted or misunderstand or basically unnecessary! These pseudolove feelings make major contributions to the problem of loneliness.

Blur of Mechanics

The third blur of true love's interdependence is the *blur of mechanics.* Mechanics have become too important! The mechanics of conversation and relationships in general are important. But when people focus on mechanics as the beginning, middle, and ending of relationships, the substance of the relationship is empty. *Mechanics, techniques, and training* instead of *life-principles, strategy, and education* rob relationships of their personness—their people-to-people interrelatedness and interdependence.

Pseudolove a Now-Love

The blurs and the blockages of pseudolove push people further into their lonely state because *pseudolove is a false love—a nonlove!* True love carries a high level of identification with the loved ones and a wish, a willingness, and an ability to reveal intimate thoughts, feelings, and sensations, as well as a general tendency toward self-disclosure. Love brings the flight of empathy, emotional understanding, and sympathetic orientation toward the loved ones. *Love is a decision to relate, confront, and encounter the loved ones honestly, frankly, and without inhibition.*[9]

Humans are less than human without other humans, and they can only become fully human when they love and are loved by other humans too. If we are to grow in our humanness, we need to love more people more deeply and more often than we do in Western society as we have created it.[10]

A father and his son were walking through the park. The little boy wanted to demonstrate his great strength to his dad, so he hovered over a large rock in order to pick it up. He said, "Look, Dad, how strong I am!" He grunted and heaved, but the rock didn't move. The boy would not easily give up. He kept trying, but was unsuccessful. His dad said, "Are you using *all* your strength?" "Yes, Dad, look at this!" Again his dad asked, "Are you sure you're using *all* your strength?" "Yes, Dad, I am, but I can't move it!" The father said, "No, son, you haven't used *all* your strength, because you haven't asked me to help you!"

The father was talking about the strength of

what true love is all about—*interdependence*. You cannot find yourself in a vacuum, but only in true love relationships.

Someone said it very clearly: *If you want to love living, you must live loving.*

8

True Love

The young man poured out his heart's devotion on paper as he wrote to the girl of his dreams:

Darling:

I love you. To prove it I would climb the highest mountain, swim the widest stream, cross the burning desert, die at the stake for you.

P.S. I will see you on Saturday—if it doesn't rain!

What kind of love is that? Our world is full of crises, but the greatest is a *love-crisis*. It's a crisis because of the mass confusion of the little four-letter word *love*. Love is one of the most overworked words in the English language; some dictionaries list as many as 25 meanings for love! Just having one word for everything leads to confusion and strange comparisons. For example, we love our lifelong sweetheart. But we also love fried chicken or quiche Lorraine, thus comparing our marriage partners of 30 years to a French cheese pie! We love our parents and our children. But we also love books or football or skiing vacations. We love freedom, surely more precious than the shiny machine in the driveway. But we *love* that new car; also we love our pets and a certain record album we bought last week. It all adds up to confusion over love—a love-crisis![1]

The love-crisis is not desperate because of linguistic reasons, but for loneliness reasons. The only positive force that will relieve the pain of loneliness is true love. People decide to be lonely, and lonely people must make another decision—*to love*. But how can you decide to love when the meaning of love is so fuzzy?

Blueprint for True Love

In searching for a definition of true love I move quickly to my philosophical base for life— the Bible. I have found the Bible to be filled with principles of life that are *true to life as it is and people as they are!*

Principles of life are true no matter what you think or believe about them. They're like the laws of nature. For example, there is the law of gravity. Stated simply, this law says that if you jump off a two-story building, you'll come down fast, with a thud, and you won't like it! It doesn't make any difference what you think or believe about it, or whether or not you like it—the law is still true. Even if the law of gravity was placed on a national ballot and voted down unanimously, the next person who attempted to jump off a two-story building would find that the law didn't know it had been voted out of existence. As he jumped, he would come down fast, with a thud, and he wouldn't like it! When you follow principles of life, you'll experience personal fulfillment. But if you ignore these principles, you'll experience everything *but* personal fulfillment.[2]

The Bible sets forth principles of life that plug people into life. Although people disagree over the Bible's authenticity and validity, there seems to be one area of almost universal acceptance. It is the familiar yet unknown area of love. The most undisputed definition and life-principles of true love are found in the Bible. The Bible offers a blueprint for true love.

The most primary passage in the Bible that defines true love is Paul's letters to the church in Corinth.

Absence of True Love

If I speak with the tongues of men and of angels, but do not have love, I have become a noisy gong or a changing cymbal. And if I have the gift of prophecy, and know all mysteries and all knowledge; and if I have all faith, so as to remove mountains, but do not have love, I am nothing. And if I give all my possessions to feed the poor, and if I deliver my

body to be burned, but do not have love,
it profits me nothing.

Presence of True Love

Love is patient, love is kind,
and is not jealous;
Love does not brag and is not arrogant,
does not act unbecomingly;
it does not seek its own,
is not provoked,
does not take into account a
wrong suffered,
does not rejoice in unrighteousness,
but rejoices with the truth;
bears all things,
believes all things,
hopes all things,
endures all things.
Love never fails.

Premanence of True Love

But if there are gifts of prophecy, they
will be done away; if there are tongues,
they will cease; if there is knowledge, it
will be done away. For we know in
part, and we prophesy in part; but
when the perfect comes, the partial will
be done away. When I was a child, I
used to speak as a child, think as a child,

reason as a child; when I became a man, I did away with childish things. For now we see in a mirror dimly, but then face to face; now I know in part, but then I shall know fully just as I have been fully known. But now abide faith, hope, love, these three; but the greatest of these is love (1 Corinthians 13:1-13).

Dynamic of True Love

There are six basic principles in the blueprint which explain the dynamic of true love. The first is best seen when love is absent: *True love fills inner vacuums.* The loneliest place in the world is the human heart when love is absent. Without love, spiritual communications ("If I speak with the tongues of men and of angels") are not important. They have become a noisy gong or a clanging cymbal. Without love, great gifts, talents, and knowledge—even powerful faith—position you as *nothing.* Without love, sacrificial gifts and martyrdom profit nothing.

Love can dynamically fill up the vacuums and fill in the gaps as needed in relationships. When things are falling apart, love can put them back together! When things go wrong, love can make them right! When people are hurt, love can heal!

The expression of love is so small and yet so powerful in its effectiveness. My wife, Carol, walks somberly into the living room and announces to me that a "nuclear blast" just blew in the back bedroom. I, in all my "wisdom and knowledge and vast counseling experience," offer her an answer to her problem in the back bedroom. As soon as I drop my "simple" answer to her problem *she turns on me!* Here I am trying to help and she is upset with *me!* You see, she really doesn't want an answer. She wants to know only one thing from me—"Do you care? Do you really care that a nuclear blast just took place in the back bedroom?" Because "If you really care, I'll go back and clean it up!" And furthermore, "If you don't care, there'll be another nuclear blast right here in the living room!" And my body will be damaged in that one! But whatever the crisis, just a little expression of love can change things dramatically.

Communication gaps existing between parents and their children can be bridged only by true love. Parents may discipline their children toward perfection, but without expression of love even consistent, proper discipline tends to push the child's rebellion button. On the other side, if parents develop a love relationship with their children but "blow it" in discipline, they will still have a good chance of being successful in parenting.

In the counseling room the absence of love is the major reason for the problem, no matter what you call it. That is why the truly successful counselor (professional or nonprofessional) communicates love for the counselee. Ninety percent of the problem is solved by the counselor's expression of love—"I care that you get through this." Why? Because *true love fills inner vacuums!*

Is Anything Totally Free?

The second basic principle in the blueprint for true love is: *True love is a free gift for the givee.* Love is primarily giving, not receiving. Love may be expressed conditionally or unconditionally. Healthy love works when love is given as an unconditional, free gift. There are no strings attached and no treadmills built. It is only in the atmosphere of unconditional, true love that the blockages can be torn down and the blurs cleared up with the relationship.

The Greek word used for love in the biblical blueprint is *agape*. Agape is an act of the will toward an unconditional expression of love. Agape love doesn't just verbalize, but mobilizes into action. It's something you do for someone. *True love must be given away!* It's a commitment toward promoting the well-being of another person.

My love must empower you to love yourself. Our success in loving is judged not by those who admire us for our accomplishments, but by the number of those who attribute their wholeness to our loving them, by the number of those who have seen their beauty in our eyes, heard their goodness acknowledged in the warmth of our voices. We are like mirrors to one another. It's an absolute certainty that no one can know his own beauty or perceive a sense of his own worth until it has been reflected back in the mirror of another loving person.[3]

As the blueprint for true love states, "love does not seek its own." It is not *self*-centered but *others*-centered! For years I wanted my wife to play the normal sports with me—like tennis, basketball, etc. I was extremely unsuccessful! She wanted to play things like hiking! To me hiking is just aimlessly wandering through the woods. But that attitude was getting nowhere.

So I decided to unselfishly love my wife in this small slice of our lives together. I came home and said, "I want to go hiking with you!" Obviously stunned, she said, "Hiking? You want to go *hiking?*" From that day forward Carol has even wanted to play some of the more normal sports! *True love does not seek its own, but seeks the best for the one loved.*

The risk in committing yourself to unconditionally loving someone is very high. You take the risk of giving love as a free, unconditional gift and not receiving anything at all in return. That's a heavy risk, and yet without such a risk there is no reward and no relief of the pain of loneliness.

Price Tag on True Love

The third basic principle is: *True love has a price tag for the giver.* The price tag is very high. For some people the price tag seems *too* high. The price tag calls for the giving of yourself. True love involves the willingness to face the inevitable pain, doubt, confrontation, misunderstanding, and dark moments within relationships. The price tag demands that you must face the relationship yourself. It demands vulnerability! People love because they are afraid of themselves, afraid of the loneliness that lives in them. People need someone in whom they can lose themselves as smoke loses itself in the sky.

To restate the principle simply: *You must lose yourself in order to find yourself—you must die to yourself in order to really live.* True love cannot happen in a vacuum but only in a relationship—an interdependent relationship. It may be the most radical principle of true love. When you give all that you are into a relationship, you mysteriously discover a more healthy *you.* Your self-image is directly connected to the quality of your relationships with others.

Whose Team Are You On?

The fourth basic principle of true love is: *True Love is affirmation, not possession.* The question is whether your love is possessive and manipulative or really affirming and freeing. Wanting what is best for another person and trying to be what that person needs you to be can be done only in a way that preserves his freedom to have his own feelings, think his own thoughts, and make his own decisions. True love is the affirmation and the celebration of an unrepeatable miracle—the uniqueness of the person loved.[4]

The biblical blueprint for true love is entirely designed to affirm. The qualities listed in 1 Corinthians 13 all seem to follow the two themes of patience (having a long fuse) and kindness (doing good toward another). Love in the form of patience is an uncommon power to cope with common suffering. Suffering itself takes no talent; it comes to us, takes us captive, pins us down. We are all its victims. Some of us have to suffer more than others. Some are able to suffer with more grace than others. But it is *love* that enables us to suffer long. It is having to endure what we very much want not to endure. On the other hand, kindness is the work of the power of love. Kindness is the will to save. It is love acting on persons. Such kindness may be soft, but it is not weak; tender, but not feeble; sensitive, but not fragile.[5]

Patience	Kindness
. . . is not jealous	. . . love does not
. . . is not provoked	brag and is not
. . . does not take into	arrogant
account a wrong	. . . does not act
suffered	unbecomingly
. . . bears all things	. . . does not seek its
. . . endures all things	own
	. . . does not rejoice
	in unrighteous-

ness, but rejoices
in the truth
. . . believes all things
. . . hopes all things
Being patient and kind toward a loved one is actually joining that person's team. And we all desperately need team members who are a reservoir of strength against the killer of loneliness.

A Taste of Foreverness

The absence of forgiveness can be devastating. Its *presence* is extremely supportive. But its *permanence* is its most distinctive characteristic. The fifth principle of true love is: *True love is a taste of eternity.* In our world of the handy, disposable "throwaways," the foreverness of love is most rare!

The biblical blueprint in 1 Corinthians 13:8-13 calls for everything as we know it to stop or run out someday. The only things in this world remaining throughout eternity are faith, hope, and agape love.

There is no time limit on love. To place a limit of any kind on love makes love conditional. The commitment of love, at whatever level, has to be permanent, a life-wager. If I say that I am your friend, I will always be your friend, not "as long as" or "until" anything. Effective love is not like the retractable point on a ball-point pen. I need to know that the love you offer me is a permanent offer before I will give up my security operations, my masks, my roles, my games. I cannot come out to a temporary, tentative love, to an offer which has all that fine print in the contract.[6]

Love Is a Full-Time Job

The final basic principle in the biblical blueprint for true love is: *True love is an active process.* No matter how romanticists have tried to color it ever-sweet, and despite the claim of cynics that it is overrated, love is the tough, essential answer to the riddle of human existence, of human wholeness and happiness. To live is to love. But if love really is the answer, it seems quite certain that the efforts of humans to find this answer in love relationships have a high mortality rate. *Love works only if people work at it!*[7]

The biblical blueprint for true love sets the standard so high that it seems humanly impossible. Unconditional, agape love is an ideal—a goal toward which true love aspires. True love requires constant work. It's a full-time job!

True love is also a process. You can never arrive. There are no push-button answers or quickie formulas or instant miracles that will switch love to a natural, automatic pilot. Most people are looking for miracles, but life is actually a process. That's what true love is all about—a lifelong process!

9

True Love: Release It!

In an Asian monastery there were very strict rules. The most unusual restriction was that each monk could only speak two words every ten years.

After Brother Barney had been in residence for ten years, he was brought in to his superior to speak his two words. "All right, Brother Barney, what are your two words?" asked the superior. Brother Barney sheepishly said, "Food, bad!"

At the end of 20 years Brother Barney was called in for his two-word interview. "What do you have to say for yourself?" Brother Barney meekly murmured, "Bed, hard!"

Now after 30 years he is called in for his third interview. This time Brother Barney angrily blurts out with, "I quit!" His superior quickly responds, "Well, I'm not surprised. All you've been doing for 30 years is complaining!"

People are lonely primarily because they are

unwilling to communicate to others. Like Brother Barney, people don't say much! Even though there are no monastic restrictions, most of us make only a weak response to the invitation of encountering others because we feel uncomfortable in our nakedness as persons.

Five Levels of Communications

Someone has delineated five levels of communication on which people can relate to one another. Each level represents a different degree of willingness to communicate. We seem to find our comfort zone on one of these levels in every relationship we encounter.

Cliches—Level 5

This level is the lowest level of communication and openness. Communication at this level is accidental at best. It consists of surfacy conversation as much as "How are you? . . . It's good to see you! . . . How is your work?" Naturally, nobody really wants an answer to these questions other than a similar surfacy response.

Actually, this is noncommunication! There is no sharing of personness at all. Everyone remains safely in the isolation of his pretense, sham, and sophistication. The whole group seems to gather to be lonely together.

Reporting Facts—Level 4

Communication on this level does not penetrate the surfacy relationship. It's just that more information is passed back and forth than in the use of cliches. Instead of any self-disclosure there is a reporting on others. Just as we hide behind cliches, so we also hide behind gossip, conversation, and little narrations about others. On this level nothing is given of ourselves and nothing from others is drawn out.

My Thoughts and Judgments—Level 3

At this level there is some communication of personness. Even though we may share ideas, judgments, and decisions, there is a strict censorship. As John Powell expresses it: "As I communicate my ideas, etc., I will be watching you carefully. I want to test the temperature of the water before I leap in. I want to be sure that you will accept me with my ideas, judgments, and decisions. If you raise your eyebrow or narrow your eyes, if you yawn or look at your watch, I will probably retreat to safer ground. I will run for the cover of silence, or change the subject of conversation, or worse, I will start to say things I suspect that you want me to say. I will try to be what pleases you."[2]

My Feelings—Level 2

Level 3 is a pure head-tripper! At level 2 we

relate much deeper and much closer to the real me. It's a shift from the head to the heart—feelings and emotions. These feelings are uniquely, personally mine. They compose the heart behind my ideas, judgments, and decisions.

Honesty is most difficult at this level! The temptation is to be dishonest on the grounds that honesty might hurt others. But real growth can take place at this level if communication is honest, open, and gut-level.

Gut Level—Level 1

Gut-level communication is for complete emotional and personal communion. It's a celebration of intimacy—the celebration of an "us!" At this level we share together, care together, laugh and cry together. It's like two musical instruments playing exactly the same note in unison or in harmony. It's the miracle of interdependence at its peak!

Decision 3—Release God's Love

The nature of loneliness, like all of our toothaches, centers the focus of attention on ourselves. As we seek to fill this vacuum and to satisfy the hunger of loneliness we normally do something very stupid: We try to manipulate people into loving us. We know that our loneliness can be relieved by the love of others. We know we must feel loved. The paradox is this: *If we seek to fill the void there is no relief, but only a deeper vacuum.* We deceive ourselves into believing that our search to be loved is loving. Most of our time and energy is spent on the prowl, looking for this experience called love. But the paradox remains; if we seek the love which we need, we will never find it.[3]

Why is this paradox so real? Because being on the prowl is not love at all. *Love can never be captured, bought, or taken. It must always be given! You must decide to actively release God's love.*

The third love-connection in the triangle is man-to-man. Plugged into a relationship with God, the source of love and life, you must now turn to developing interdependent relationships on the human level. To release God's love I suggest six action steps.

Exposing

Expose yourself! *Tell the truth about yourself!* We resist self-disclosure. We want a place of safety, barricaded against the invasion of others with their probing questions and inquisitive desire to know all about us. There is no nakedness more painful than psychological nakedness. This need for safety and self-protection breeds a deadly myth. The myth is that everyone needs his own private retreat where no one else can enter. It sounds good and is most popular, but it is only an exercise in wishful thinking. Rather than a place reserved exclusively for self, what we really need is to have someone (a total confidant) know us completely and some others (close friends) know us very deeply. The pockets of privacy which we create for a place to run where no one can follow us are death to the kind of human intimacy so necessary to the fullness of human life.[4]

In his book *The Transparent Self,* psychologist Sidney Jourard relates some illuminating studies about the subject of self-disclosure. His major finding is that the human personality has a natural, built-in inclination to reveal itself. When that inclination is blocked and we close ourselves to others, we get into emotional difficulties. This is why the most frequent expression heard by the counselor (professional or amateur) is "You are the first person I have ever been completely open and honest with!"[5]

We have the ambivalent feelings of longing to be known and understood on the one hand and desiring to remain hidden and covered up on the other. Therefore, we build walls between relationships instead of bridges to link relationships together. All the masks of loneliness come to our aid as we run from exposing ourselves.

The brilliant Swiss psychiatrist Carl Jung advised his patients to become acquainted with what he called the "shadow side" of themselves, or the "inferior part of the personality." There is a hidden portion of our minds that is comprised of memories from the past which terrify us and of which we are ashamed, plus the mean, selfish, and base nature which erupts occasionally and which we try to excuse and explain away in a thousand different ways. The natural assumption is that if we let others see this dark side, they will be turned away or even hate us. But generally, they are able to be more emphathetic and understanding with us than we are with ourselves. A curious kind of chemistry starts to work. Through telling another person the truth about ourselves, we begin to understand ourselves better. It's the principle of losing yourself in order to find yourself![6]

Two cautions should be heeded as you take the risk of exposing yourself. The first is the extreme of telling the truth about yourself to *just anyone,* or even to someone special *all at once.* Choose your confidants carefully and expose yourself gradually. The second caution is to tell the truth *about yourself—not about others.* There is a natural tendency as it becomes easier to open up to do some "mind-reading" and "fortune-telling"—trying to tell what you believe to be the truth about others. You are only responsible for your self-disclosure. You cannot self-disclose someone else; it's nothing more than psychological rape!

Emoting

The second action step in releasing love is by

expressing your gut-level emotions. This is emoting!

Emotions are not moral. Both good and bad emotions are O.K. They are simply factual and must be reported. Feeling frustrated, or being annoyed, or experiencing fears and anger do not make a person good or bad.

If our emotions are not *reported,* they will be *repressed.* If our censoring consciences do not approve certain emotions, we repress these emotions into our subconscious mind. Experts in psychosomatic medicine say that the most common cause of fatigue and actual sickness is through the repression of emotions.[7]

Instead of repressing, report your emotions! If you feel angry, sad, disappointed, or guilty, report these feelings as your feelings. If I am to tell you who I am, I must tell you about my feelings, whether I will act upon them or not. I may tell you that I am angry, explaining the fact of my anger without incurring any judgment by you, and not intending to act upon this anger. I may tell you that I am afraid, explaining the fact of my fear without accusing you of being its cause, and at the same time not being overwhelmed by the fear. But I must, if I am to expose myself to you, allow you to experience my person and report to you my anger and my fear.[8]

As much as is possible, emotions should be reported on the spot—right at the time you are feeling them. The balance of when, how, and to whom you report your emotions must be carefully juggled. Count on making mistakes, and when you do, report that emotion as well! This balancing act of properly reporting your feelings as you check in with your mind is all part of processing your emotions instead of dangerously repressing them. When you repress your feelings, you will inevitably pay for it in your gut!

Be careful not to spill your guts in every relationship. It's impossible to relate to everyone on the most intimate, number-one gut level. All kinds of people may desire a more intimate relationship with you, but you could do nothing else. In some ways, it sounds good, even mature, to be able to relate to everyone on the number-one level. To be *able* to relate on that level is mature, but to attempt this with everyone is immature and idealistic. There is no magic number of people for you to include on the number-one level of relationships. But a good guideline is to relate to at least two on this intimate level. Some can handle more than 20, and others feel most comfortable with four or five, but you cannot afford to have less than two!

Judging

It is said that the favorite indoor sport of most churches is confessing the sins of others!

Condemning other people's actions and feelings is the exact opposite of the biblical blueprint for true love. Condemnatory judgment expects to find fault and enjoys criticism for its own sake. It's one of the most destructive of all things as you attempt to release love within a relationship.

So why do I say that *by judging* you take another step in the act of releasing love? There are two basic definitions of judgment. One is *to condemn* (as described above). The other is *to conclude*—to esteem, to determine, to think. Only God can justly condemn someone. But man must make conclusions; he must judge by conclusion. When the conclusion kind of judgment is understood and practiced, relationships become more clarified, honest, and open.

But why are we to judge, even by conclusion, in our relationships? What does judging have to do with releasing love to another? You see, judging in the right kind of spirit is a critical ingredient in loving. Loving another person always involves face-to-face confrontation. To avoid the pain and uneasiness of confrontation in a love relationship is not to love at all! The wise man Solomon put it this way: "An open rebuke is better than love in secret." Caring enough to confront means that you are willing to risk being misunderstood as you admonish, warn, disagree, or rebuke a loved one. A true friend/lover will express his conclusions about you because he loves you. A person who is unwilling to tell you when you have food on your face is not releasing love to you.

Obviously, since judging in the spirit of conclusion is meant to be an act of love, then the whole process of confronting can only happen within the context of a secure love relationship. In other words, when you judge in this way you must be sure to communicate your unconditional love.

David Augsburger, in his practical *Caring Enough to Confront,* encourages confrontation when the proper context exists. Giving another person feedback on how he or she is coming on can be surprisingly simple when it is offered in a context of caring, supportive acceptance; it can be astoundingly difficult when interpreted as intensive, nonsupportive rejection.

Hearing confrontation from another person is no problem when we are certain that the other person respects, values, and cares for us in spite of all the differences between us; but when respect is unclear and caring is unexpressed, we can feel fed up with another's feedback before it even begins.

Caring comes first, then confrontation follows. A context of caring can be created when a person is truly *for* another person, genuinely concerned about another, authentically related to another. The content of such caring is, however, not a blank-check approval of the other. The core of true caring is a clear invitation to grow, to become what he or she truly is and can be, and to move toward maturity. Accepting, appreciating, valuing another person is an important part of relationship, but these attitudes may or may not be caring. The crucial elements are: Does it foster growth? Does it invite maturing? Does it set another person more free? Is it truly an expression of love?

A context of caring must come before
   confrontation.
A sense of support must be present
   before criticism.
An experience of empathy must
   precede evaluation.
A basis of trust must be laid before one
   risks advising.
A floor of affirmation must undergird
   any assertiveness.
A gift of understanding opens the way
   to disagreeing.
An awareness of love sets us free to
   level with each other.

Building solidarity in relationships with others—through caring, support, empathy, trust, affirmation, understanding, and love—provides a foundation for the more-powerful actions of confrontation, criticism, evaluation, counsel, assertiveness, disagreement, and open leveling with each other.[9]

The biblical blueprint for judging with the spirit of conclusion has been greatly misunderstood:

Do not judge lest you be judged. For in the way you judge, you will be judged; and by your standard of measure, it will be measured to you.

And why do you look at the speck that is in your brother's eye but do not notice the log that is in your own eye? Or how can you say to your brother, "Let me take the speck out of your eye," and behold, the log is in your own eye? You hypocrite, first take the log out of your own eye, and then you will see clearly to take the speck out of your brother's eye.[10]

Most people use this section of the biblical blueprint to justify that we are never to judge at all. But it is expressing just the opposite! "Do not judge lest you be judged" is a Hebrew idiom which says that we are to *judge ourselves first*. Judging with the spirit of conclusion demands a proper starting point—*you*! When you make a conclusion kind of judgment, you set yourself as an authority. And as that authority you will be judged by the same standard you use in judging others. It only makes sense to start by looking into the mirror.

There are two problems when a conclusion judgment is made improperly. The first is the problem of credibility. How can you look at the speck that is in your brother's eye when you do not notice the log that is in your own eye? How can you confront a friend about something in his life while you are guilty of the same thing? It's a pretense of being moral and righteous. Without removing the log in your own eye, your action quickly loses credibility.

The second is the problem of effectiveness.

How can you say to your brother, "Let me take the tiny speck out of your eye" when you have a large log in your own eye? It's a pretense of being able to help. With that log in your eye you cannot be effective in removing the speck out of your brother's eye! You can't see clearly enough to help.

Judging properly includes two simple steps—be a log remover, then be a speck remover. A little girl visiting her grandmother was helping out by dusting the dining room table. When her grandmother inspected the table she said, "That's good, honey, but there is a large area in the middle of the table that you missed!" The little girl redusted the table and announced her accomplishment. Again her grandmother inspected the table. "You still haven't dusted that area right in the middle of the table!" Again the little girl dusted diligently and again her grandmother chastised her for her poor dusting job. Exasperated, the little girl realized what was happening. She blurted out, "Grandma, the dust is not on the table. It's on your glasses!" *Be a log-remover before you become a speck-remover.*

Forgiving

Someone said, "I have forgiven and forgotten, and I don't want you to forget that I have forgiven and forgotten!" That's not pure forgiveness. Because of the various weaknesses and mistakes within people, forgiveness is absolutely necessary for love to be released. When you are wronged or hurt by your loved one, you have a few choices. You can try *retaliation* for the purpose of repayment for your hurt. But repayment is impossible. You can try *revenge*, but revenge is ineffective. Revenge not only lowers you to your "enemy's" level, but it boomerangs. The person who seeks revenge is like the man who shoots himself in order to hit his "enemy" with the kick of the gun's recoil. You can also try *resentment*. But resentment not only hurts others; resentment hurts you even more.[11]

There is an interesting dynamic in the act of forgiving. Throughout the biblical blueprint there is a couplet—*forgive so that you might be forgiven*. Unless you forgive, you will not be forgiven.

The whole package of forgiveness sets you free from the three most basic psychological problems of fear, anger, and guilt. Experiencing forgiveness through a relationship with God gives the power to eliminate the core problem of *fear*. On the horizontal, human level, when you forgive you experience freedom from your *anger* and resentment. And when you are forgiven by another person, you are set free from your *guilt*.

But what is forgiveness? How does it work? Forgiveness begins with 1) *respect for otherness*. You must give the freedom to your loved one to be different from you. This includes strengths as well as weaknesses. It's the freedom to succeed and the freedom to fail— *the freedom to be.* Then, forgiveness means 2) *differentiate between your offender and the offense.* It is possible to hate the offense and yet love the offender. You must separate the two in order to forgive.

Forgiveness also involves 3) *being willing to hurt in order to heal.* Since repayment is really impractical and most ineffective, someone must bear the hurt. When you choose to forgive, you are also choosing to be the sufferer in order for healing to take place within the relationship. To forgive is to make a heavy love—commitment!

To help the healing process, 4) *giving a blessing* is necessary. Giving a blessing can be a gift, but verbalization is most effective. It is genuinely expressing thankfulness and praise for qualities you appreciate in the other person. Love itself is revolutionary, but love's expression through giving a blessing in reaction to a hurt is the most rare of all.

Finally, forgiveness requires 5) *forgetting the offense.* To begin the process of forgiving with trying to forget makes it all worse. Forgetting is the *result* of complete forgiveness; it is never the *means.* It is the *final* step, not the *first* step.

There is no forgiveness in the cheap little game of looking the other way when a wrong is done. Forgiveness never just overlooks or winks at a wrong. It does not make light of the offense. It is no bit of pious pretending that an offense is not really an offense. Forgiveness is not mere politeness, tact, or diplomacy! Nor is it just forgetting. You will forget after you truly forgive. But to insist that forgetting comes first is to make passing the final exam the entrance requirement for the course. The person who struggles to forget without going through the prior steps of forgiveness only sears the thought more deeply into his memory.

Touching

The fifth action step in releasing God's love is *to touch!* Our society dwells in two extremes. On one hand we distance ourselves from people without a healthy relationship. On the other hand we jump into sexual relationships without a healthy relationship. Some are paranoid about any physical contact. Others are obsessed with the physical urge to merge.

Somewhere between these extremes is the healthy balance. It's learning to release love by touching! Touching is the coup de grace of communications. If you view man as a spiritual, emotional, and physical being, you can appreciate the magnitude of this expression. Touching is the one communication form that ties all three dimensions into one. Because we are in part physical beings, we need to relate to our world through touch from the time of birth. For infants the need for touch is so great that they literally cannot survive without it.

Through this sense mechanism, early feelings of warmth, security, and comfort begin to grow.[12]

Love released by touching is an act of tenderness and warmth. Loving tenderness is a need that all people have, and yet in American culture such expression is often discouraged. Grace Stuart explains in a passage from *Narcissus:* "It is too seldom mentioned that the baby, being quite small for quite a long time, is a handled creature, handled and held. The touch of hands on the body is one of the first and last of physical experiences, and we deeply need that it be tender. We want to touch . . . and a culture that has placed a taboo on tenderness leaves us stroking our dogs and cats when we may not stroke each other. We want to be touched . . . and often we dare not say so . . . . We are starved for the laying on of hands."[13]

When counseling children caught in the middle of a divorce, the concept of love released through physical touch is most clear. One of the goals in these cases is to assure the children of their parents' love for them. The counselor's question may be, "you know your dad loves you, don't you?" Invariably the child's response is, "Yeah, my dad wrestles with me!" or "I know, because he tickles me!" or "He dunks me in the pool!" *Love is magically released and effectively communicated through touching.*

During the nineteenth century more than half of the infants died in their first year of life from a diseased called *marasmus*, a Greek word meaning "wasting away." As late as the 1920s, according to Montagu, the death rate for infants under one year of age in various U.S. foundling institutions was close to 100 percent! A distinguished New York pediatrician, Dr. Chapin, noted that the infants were kept in sterile, neat, tidy wards, but were rarely picked up. Chapin brought in women to hold the babies, coo to them, and stroke them, and the mortality rate dropped drastically. Just like the babies, millions of lonely people are sick and dying because of the lack of warmth and tenderness—much of it through touch![14]

One caution is appropriate here: *Physical gushing is as offensive as verbal gushing.* But when it is a genuine expression of your love, touch can bring you closer to another person than can thousands of words. Men can find masculine ways of giving a loving message to other men. Get into the habit of shaking hands. The act of your going to the person and getting the close proximity of your bodies necessary for the handshake conveys a message. A pat on the back, a playful pinch in the stomach, "Give me five!" or your hand on a man's shoulder as you talk—all these should make up your vocabulary of gestures. In our contacts with the opposite sex, touching need not always have a sexual connotation. We can give encouragement, offer comfort, or express tenderness with physical demonstrations.[15]

Love by touching communicates "I affirm you!" or "I care about you!"

Initiating

The final suggested action step for releasing love in a relationship is sort of all-encompassing. It is releasing love *by initiating love.* We all need love from others, but to be lovable we must be lovers—initiating love!

This initiation of love cannot be based on the feeling of obligation:

Obligation says:	**Love says:**
"I must because I owe it."	"I will because I choose to."
"I should because it's expected of me."	"I want to because I care."
"I ought to because I'm supposed to."	"I'd like to."

The initiation of love requires that you love yourself first. The biblical blueprint says, "Love your neighbor as yourself!" The corollary to this principle is, "If you don't love yourself, then your neighbor is in a heap of trouble!" Self-love is usually mistaken for selfishness. But they are miles apart. Selfishness is destructive. Self-love is the first step toward initiating love's release. It is interesting to note that one of the most critical steps in relieving the pain of loneliness is to develop love for myself all *alone.*

There is a growing consensus of opinion that there is one need so fundamental and so essential that if it is met, everything else will almost certainly harmonize in a general sense of well-being. When this need is properly nourished, the whole human organism will be healthy and the person will be happy. This need is a true and deep love of self, a genuine and joyful self-acceptance, an authentic self-esteem, which result in an interior sense of celebration: "It's good to be me . . . . I am very happy to be me!"[17]

Instead of waiting around for the love of others, the decision to release God's love calls for your initiation. You want to feel loved, then to love. The power of love is phenomenal when unleashed. That power is so effective that the biblical blueprint directs the loving of your enemies.

Years ago I was having a real problem loving a man who worked with me. He was just repulsive to me. It occurred to me that he was like an enemy. Therefore, my relationship with him needed some initiation on my part— *like love!* Just like loneliness, love is a decision. It's a decision to do something good for someone. So I began my release of love toward this young man. I took him to lunch. I challenged him to a tennis game. I basically focused my attention on appreciating and encouraging him. An amazing thing happened. This guy changed dramatically! I even began to like him. But you know, he didn't change. Not really. I was the one who was changed through the powerful release of love—*by initiating love!*

10

From Loneliness to Love

Everybody is lonely! It seems the more I say it the more I realize its overwhelming penetration. Daily I see people entangled in the web of loneliness. People may become lonely through all kinds of circumstances (active and passive), but it is a fact that everyone experiences the problem and its pain.

Loneliness is driving people crazy!

Loneliness is terrorizing the family unit!

Loneliness actually kills millions of people each year!

Loneliness is a taste of hell!

We are all lonely in varying degrees. I have researched loneliness extensively, I have counseled people through it, and I am now writing this book on the subject, but I still experience degrees of loneliness. Even after reading this book, you will still be lonely! Just the writing or reading of a book on loneliness will not bring about significant relief from its pain.

Even though it acts like a disease (causes discomfort, sickness, and death), loneliness is not a disease. It's a decision! Loneliness is a decision based upon the fear of love. We are lonely because of our fear of love. This is the foundational fear which underlies *the fear or identity* (the love of who you are), *the fear of inadequacy* (the fear of what you do), and *the fear of intimacy* (the love of others).

Since loneliness is a decision and not a disease, there is hope! If a decision or series of decisions made me lonely (or intensified my loneliness), then a decision or series of decisions can relieve my loneliness. *The decision to uncover loneliness with all of its masquerades* (depression, anxiety, guilt, anger, heart disease, cancer, etc.) *is the decision to love!*

Double-Edged Decision

It's a double-edged decision—a decision to relieve your loneliness and a decision to release your love. It's a package deal! When you decide to relieve your loneliness, you must also decide to release your love. You cannot stop with only one action, but each necessitates the other. Anything short of the double-edged decision is incomplete.

There is an old joke which goes, "When is a door not a door?" The answer is, "When it's ajar!" But the true meaning should go as follows: "When is a door not a door?" "When it is something else." When is a liar not a liar? Certainly not when he stops lying, but when he stops lying and starts telling the truth. When is a thief not a thief? Is it when he quits stealing? No way! He may just be between jobs! It's when he stops stealing and starts working and giving! The same kind of double-edged decision is necessary when moving from loneliness to love.

Perpetual Decision

Life continues to change. People move, die, shift jobs, separate, divorce, etc. Very little remains the same. These variable circumstances force us into loneliness from time to time without any direct decision being made. When a loved one dies or deserts you, loneliness is the result. You did not choose it, but you have it just the same.

With this in mind, it is important to realize that *one* double-edged decision to relieve my loneliness and to release my love will not keep me forever free from loneliness. Instead, I must perpetually decide *against* loneliness and *for* love. Life is filled with cycles of going in and out of loneliness. In other words, you will periodically visit the state of loneliness, but you do not have to live there.

People Decision

So many people try to relieve their loneliness

through a change of scenery, a change of job or position, or the purchase of new "toys" (clothes, jewelry, a boat, a plane, a car). All these will help to relieve the pain of loneliness— temporarily!

The decision from loneliness to love has nothing to do with prosperity, possessions, or playthings. This decision is a people decision. Only other people can fill the loneliness vacuum, and only other people can interconnect with your love!

Possible Decision

The decision to move from loneliness to love may be difficult, but it is possible. Because of the difficulty, it is so easy to victimize yourself through the simple words, "I can't!" "I can't" is not the truth. "I can't" really means "I won't!" It isn't that you "can't" make the decision, because it's possible. More than likely the motivation to do something about the loneliness is not strong enough to move you to action.

This motivation predicament reminds me of the rabbit who was stuck in a hole. He scream-ed for help with everything he could muster. A frog heard his cry for help and hopped over to the rabbit as quickly as he could. "What's the matter, Mr. Rabbit?" "I'm stuck in this hole and I can't get out!" "Don't worry, Mr. Rabbit," said the frog, "I'll get a ladder and help you out of that hole!"

The frog hurried as fast as he could and brought a ladder back to help the rabbit out of his predicament. When he arrived back at the scene, Mr. Rabbit was happily standing outside the hole. "I thought you said you couldn't get out of that hole," said Mr. Frog. Mr. Rabbit quickly explained, "Well, *I couldn't*, but a snake crawled into the other end of this hole and *I did*."

When the motivation is high enough, the decision becomes possible. As soon as I realize what loneliness was doing to me and could do, I was sufficiently motivated to do whatever possible to deactivate this killer.

Moving to Love

Let's capitalize the "how to" of escaping loneliness and expressing love.

1. Remember that loneliness is not a disease—it's a decision!

    A *double-edged decision*—you relieve your loneliness by releasing your love.

    A *perpetual decision*—once you have decided to relieve your loneliness by releasing your love, your loneliness problem is not over. Through other circumstances it will most likely appear again and again. Each time you face it, deal with it by making the proper decisions!

A *people decision*—do not expect property, possessions, or playthings to relieve your pain of loneliness on a long-term basis; they are only temporary distractions. Only people can effectively relieve your loneliness.

A *possible decision*—no matter what the circumstances, you can decide against loneliness and for love. The question is not *can* you do it but *will* you!

2. *Release your love and relieve your loneliness!*

Try the following six action steps in expressing your love to another person. However, do not try them all at once. Start with the one with which you feel most comfortable.

Go back and reread Chapter 9 to more fully understand what to do. Focus on it in your relationship for a full weekend, and watch the difference it makes in releasing your love. Whatever you do to apply these six action steps, the important thing is to do something!

1. Love by *exposing* yourself. Tell the truth about yourself. Find a trustworthy confidant and open up.

2. Love by *emoting*. Instead of repressing, report your emotions. If you feel sad, angry, disappointed, or

guilty, report these feelings as *your* feelings.

3. Love by *judging*. Don't *condemn* others but *confront* others. Within the atmosphere of unconditional love you must *care* enough to *confront* the person with food on his/her face.

4. Love by *forgiving*. Instead of retaliation, revenge, or resentment, try forgiving. This separates the offense from the offender so that you can hate what was done but still love the doer. This may be the most dynamic action step of love ever attempted.

5. Love by *touching*. When it is a genuine expression of love, touch can bring you closer to another person than can thousands of words. Touching does not need to always have a sexual connotation. You can give encouragement, offer comfort, or express warmth and tenderness through touching. Love is magically released and effectively communicated just by touching!

6. Love by *initiating*. It is said that the entire sum of existence is the magic of being needed by just one person.

We all need love from others, but to
be lovable we must first be lovers—
initiating love!

Today you can begin moving out of loneliness into love. You *can* do it! Now you *must* do
it! From now on, *it's your move*!

Appendix I

Perfect Love

The year: 2000 A.D.

The place: the world's most advanced center of computer technology.

The occasion: the unveiling of the Ultimate Computer, at last able to do instant, infinite calculations on abstract questions.

Of the many stockpiled questions awaiting answers, one has been selected as the forerunner of all time.

"Is there a God?"

The computer warms its circuits, then speaks the answer in its synthetic monotone: "If there was no God before, there is now!"

If we finally create our own all-knowing deities, making gods to ourselves in our own image, we will not be at their mercy, for the technological god cannot offer mercy. No matter how wonderfully computers may revolutionize our lives, there will always be one great lack—no love, loveless logic! Who could expect mercy, love, or forgiveness from the cold gray steel of a mechanical system like that?

Who could live in a computerized world except perfect people stereotyped after an ideal IBM card-punch pattern?[1]

Love cannot be found within the inner workings of computer machinery. Love is discovered only in people-to-people relationships. People-to-people love is riddled with holes—weaknesses and failures. But there is a more complete love that is tied to eternity. It's the source, the energy, behind all true love. It's *perfect love*! It's God! Perfect love is rooted in God.

Perfect Love: The Ultimate Love-Connection

Jesus was asked an interesting question about the essence of God's commandments: "Teacher, which is the great commandment in the Law?"

And He said to him, "*You shall love the Lord your God with all your heart, and with all your soul, and with all your mind.* This is the great and foremost commandment. The second is like it, *You shall love your neighbor as yourself.* On these two commandments depend the whole Law and the Prophets."[2]

The theme of God's communication to man is love! All other principles of life rest upon this foundational theme. Perfect love is the only dynamic that can possibly reach down inside the core of man's loneliness and ease the pain. Perfect love is the only possible force that can remove the fears of identity, inadequacy, and intimacy which separate us from each other. Perfect love also has the power to remove the spin-off problems of fear—anger and guilt!

But what is perfect love? *Perfect love is the ultimate love-connection!* It's a triangular connection of God's love for man, man's love for God, and man's love for man. The biblical blueprint for perfect love is written in 1 John 4:7-21. The blueprint begins with a summary statement of the triangular love-connection:

Beloved, let us love one another, for love is from God; and everyone who loves [man-to-man] is born of God [God-to-man] and knows God [man-to-God].[3]

It Works Best When It's Plugged In!

In Chapter 5 we saw that man as he is now is abnormal. He is not O.K.! The alienation, depersonalization, fears, and pains within man are not O.K. Since man is abnormal, there is hope for positive change—to move back toward normality. The only hope for man is to be plugged back into his Creator. You see, *man works best when he's plugged in!* In order to experience perfect love and begin to eliminate loneliness we must plug into the triangular connection.

Decision 1—Receive God's Love

Loneliness is not a disease; it's a decision! In fact, loneliness is the product of several decisions. After counseling thousands of lonely people, I'm convinced that there are three vital decisions which *best* transform the hollowness.

The three decisions are: 1) *receive* God's love; (2) *reciprocate* God's love; and 3) *release* God's love. Although the first two are more continual, examine carefully all three on your way out of loneliness into love.

The first decision relates to the connection of God to man. It is the decision to receive God's love! The biblical blueprint for perfect love explains this connection of a relationship with God.

By this I am not referring to religion, but a *relationship with God*. Religion with its system of do's and don't is a massive turn-off. When I wanted my ticket to get into heaven, I was handed a list of 12 things that you don't do in order to get your ticket. As I carefully examined that list I realized that those were my goals in life!

> The one who does not love does not know God, for God is love. By this the love of God was manifested in us, that God has sent His only begotten Son into the world so that we might live through Him.

> In this is love, not that we loved God, but that He loved us and sent His Son to be the propitiation [satisfaction] for our sins. Beloved, if God so loved us, we also ought to love one another. No one has

beheld God at any time; if we love one another, God abides in us, and *His love is perfected in us.*

And we have come to know and have believed the love which God has for us. *God is love,* and the one who abides in love abides in God, and God abides in him. By this, *love is perfected with us,* that we may have confidence in the day of judgment; because as He is, so also are we in this world! *There is no fear in love; but perfect love casts out fear,* because fear involves punishment, *and the one who fears is not perfected in love. We love because He first loved us.*[4]

In the gut of every human being is a vacuum. In this vacuum are all the feelings of alienation and depersonalization—the fears and pains which prevent the uninhibited flow of love in relationships. These fears must be cast out. *Perfect love casts out fear because there is no fear in love!*

Perfect love cannot be found in merely people-to-people relationships. Attempts have been made from the beginning of time to establish perfect love, but failure is inevitable. Perfect love is only experienced as people are reconnected to the God of the universe.

Perfect love is a complete kind of love, and the first connection of God's love toward man creates the foundation for all facets of loving. The first decision, then is: *receive God's love!*

Anyone can experience true love, but *perfect love* occurs only through being connected to God's love. You can fight loneliness without perfect love, but I'm convinced that you will not ultimately be successful.

To receive God's love is to receive His action to reconnect you back to Himself—to make you O.K. again by offering forgiveness to everyone. Man's sin or self-centered rebellion is against God. The attitude is: "God, You go Your way and I'll go mine. Check with me when I'm 76 or 77 and we'll negotiate!" Man's sin must be paid for by death. So God sent His Son to die for us. This was God's love gift! You pay nothing. God pays everything. You get God and God gets you!

A gift is not yours unless you receive it. In man's innermost psyche he feels he must pay for what he has done wrong. He does this by "shooting" himself into a depression. Some people try to kill themselves as an ultimate payment for failure. God's Son died to make a payment in our place, so that we don't have to pay anymore. Receiving God's love is actually receiving His forgiveness for our offenses! As a lonely person I need to know I'm loved and forgiven for all my failures by the One who really counts—God Himself. But it's not mine unless I *receive* it—accept it as my own.

The mind-boggling thought about God's love is that God will not love you any more next week than He does now! There is nothing you can do to earn God's love. It's a free gift!

Another overwhelming fact is that once you receive God's love and forgiveness you cannot be separated from it again.

> Who shall separate us from the love of Christ? Shall tribulation, or distress, or persecution, or famine, or nakedness, or peril, or sword . . . ? But in all these we overwhelmingly conquer through Him who loved us. For I am convinced that neither death, nor life, nor angels, nor principalities, nor things present, nor things to come, nor powers, nor height, not depth, nor any other created thing shall be able to separate us from the love of God, which is Christ Jesus our Lord.[5]

Perfect love is rooted in God and becomes the foundation for true love. As the blueprint puts it: *We love because He first loved us.*

Decision 2—Reciprocate God's Love

Perfect love involves receiving God's love and reciprocating God's love before I can engage in loving others. The decision to reciprocate God's love triggers an interesting and almost mysterious dynamic. The biblical blueprint for perfect love expresses the second connection of man to God.

> If someone says "I love God" and hates his brother, he is a liar; for the one who does not love his brother, whom he has

seen, cannot love God, whom he has not
seen. And this commandment we have
from Him, that the one who loves God
should love his brother also.[6]

*One of the greatest roadblocks to loving
others and the greatest contributor to loneliness is self-centeredness.* When our focus is
turned inward, it is impossible to give ourselves effectively to much of anything. When
turned inward we wallow with the friends of
loneliness: guilt, anger, resentment, depression, physical pains, pity, and pride. But if we
can focus outside ourselves there is a freedom
to break out of our spell of loneliness into the
activity of love.

When things were getting rough for Jesus
and His disciples, Peter, the most vocal of the
group, temporarily turned traitor by repeated-
ly denying that he ever knew Jesus. Jesus was
tried and executed by crucifixion. During the
trial and execution you can imagine the guilt
and anxiety that Peter must have experienced.
But then something happened that caused
Peter even more stress: Jesus was resurrected!
It's one thing to feel guilty, but it's quite
another thing to have to *face* the person you
have wronged!

I know the feeling well. Somehow when you
are about to face up to the confrontation, the
stomach moves to the throat and choking
begins. Peter found himself at a campfire sit-
ting right next to Jesus. No doubt Peter expected Jesus to reprimand him in some way

and demand an apology. But Jesus surprised Peter; He didn't say a thing against Peter and didn't demand any kind of an apology. Instead, He asked Peter an amazing question!

Jesus leans toward Peter. Peter's stomach moves to his throat, and choking begins. Jesus asks, "Do you love me, Peter?" Peter is pleasantly surprised and quickly answers, "Yes, Lord, you know I love you!" But Jesus did not accept his answer as adequate, because He asked Peter the same question twice more.[7]

Whatever else could be said about the confrontation between Jesus and Peter, the action step offered to Peter, who was weighted down by his loneliness, is a dynamic insight into handling this kind of problem. Instead of having Peter undo his loneliness and guilt or offer him something for the pain, *Jesus moved him toward the triangular connection of perfect love.* First Jesus approached Peter with love and acceptance in the way he confronted him. It's not so much *what He said* that displays this love but *what He didn't say*! This is the God-to-man connection. Second, Jesus was drawing Peter into the man-to-God connection by focusing on Peter's love for the God-man rather than on his inward focus of despair. He pulled Peter out of himself. This shift then freed Peter for expressing love outwardly. Finally, after Peter experienced and expressed God's love and his love for God, Jesus instructed him toward loving others by caring for them. This is the third link in the triangular love-connection—man-to-man.

Through receiving and reciprocating God's love, Peter plugged himself into life. As he got out of himself into a relationship with God, Peter was finally free to be human—to celebrate his personness! He was free from the paralyzing fears of identity, inadequacy, and intimacy. He was free to discover his identity, to demonstrate his adequacy, and to develop intimacy in relationships. Peter decided not to be lonely, with all its accompanying problems.

Once you have plugged into perfect love, you are even better able to move on to where the "nitty" gets "gritty"—the decision to release God's love in relationships!

Appendix II

When You Need a
Faith Lift

Loneliness is primarily in relationship (or lack of relationship) with people. But the temperature of a lonely person is measured not only by the people who let him down but also by the circumstances which get him down. Just as you must initiate relieving your loneliness as you relate to people, so you must take responsibility to respond properly as you relate to circumstances.

When Trials Come

The whole idea of a faith lift is what you do when trials come. What do you do when you're lying in the hospital with tubes coming out of your body—out of more places than you thought you had places, where blood is going in and blood is going out, where they are sticking you every few minutes to wake you up to give you another shot? That is when you need a faith lift.

When you've got a family situation where your children have gone berserk on you, even though they were lovely little things at one point in time, that's when you need a faith lift.

You get to the point where you think you're rocking along very well. Your job is secure and everything is going well. Then all of a sudden somebody turns the faucet off. You lose your job; your house burns down; you wreck your car; relationships are falling apart. That's when you need a faith lift.

All of us face trials. You go through a marital struggle in which you are having difficulty communicating. You are trying desperately to just get through to that crazy person you live with. That's when you need a faith lift. These trials and struggles are with people and things. When people and circumstances get you down, you need a faith lift!

When you need a faith lift the key is to re-focus away from the trials themselves. It seems natural for us to focus on the trials. "How are you doing?" "Oh, you shouldn't have asked! Let me *tell* you how I'm doing." As one person put it, "When you brood over your trials, you hatch despair and depression and disintegration of your own self." Many people have ulcers today because they are mountain-climbing over molehills. They've got this little pile over here and they finally get up and say, "I think I'm going to scale this one," when all you have to do is step over it or maybe scoop it out of the way. They are mountain-climbing over molehills. "How are you doing?" "Oh my, it's bad." They have faces long enough to eat popcorn out of a milk bottle! Here is what the biblical blueprint says about handling trials:

Consider it all joy, my brethren, when you encounter various trials, knowing that the testing of your faith produces endurance. And let endurance have its perfect result, that you may be perfect and complete, lacking in nothing.

But if any of you lacks wisdom, let him ask of God, who gives to all men generously and without reproach, and it will be given to him. But let him ask in faith, without any doubting, for the one who doubts is like the surf of the sea, driven and tossed by the wind. For let not that man expect that he will receive anything from the Lord, being a double-minded man, unstable in all his ways.

But let the brother of humble circumstances glory in his high position; and let the rich man glory in his humiliation, because like flowering grass he will pass away. For the sun rises with a scorching wind and withers the grass, and its flower falls off and the beauty of its appearance is destroyed; so too the rich man in the midst of his pursuits will fade away.

Blessed is a man who perseveres under trial, for once he has been approved he will receive the crown of life, which the Lord has promised to those who love Him. Let no one say when he is tempted, "I am being tempted by God"; For God cannot be tempted by evil, and He Himself does not tempt anyone (James 1:2-13).

Everytime you focus on the trials or who caused the trials you move into a victim syndrome. Victims are seldom aware of what is happening. They comfortably crawl under their piles of life hoping that their problems will go away. You blame things. You blame people. You blame your mother. You blame your dad. You blame that person way back in your life that really messed you up and now you're paying for it. You blame your boss, you blame your wife, you blame your husband, you blame your kids. But whatever you do, don't blame yourself! When you need a faith lift, playing the victim role will not help. It perpetuates itself! You must refocus from the trials!

There are two basic words in the Greek language that would be translated "trials" or "testing." One is when you are trying to test someone with a view toward negative results. You want to trip him up. That is where we get the word "tempt." You are tempting him to do wrong. But there is another Greek word with the meaning that I am going to test you with a view toward approval—a positive result. I am going to give you a test to show you that you have been refined as gold. I am going to give you this test to prove your genuineness. One test is out to prove that you are not genuine, that you are false. The other is out to prove that you are genuine.

Rejoice in the Product

With these words in mind I want to give you three ways to refocus when you need a faith lift. *The first is by rejoicing in the product that the trials will produce.* Rejoicing in the product! "Consider it all joy, my brethren, when you encounter various trials, knowing that the testing of your faith produces endurance. And let endurance have its perfect result, that you may be perfect by complete, lacking in nothing."

God does not try to make you do evil or try to trip you up. God does not throw things at you so that you will trip up and mess up and fall apart. A lot of people teach today that everything that comes into your life is of God. It is of God in one sense—that God allowed that to come into your life and through that horrible thing that just came into your life, here's what is going to happen. He says, "Count it all joy when you encounter various trials—outward trials that you can't do anything about—

knowing that the testing of your faith will produce something good and positive." He will use this trial that was meant for evil to bring about good. He will produce the good quality of endurance. I think the best word to translate this word "endurance" is *perseverance.* He is saying, "Count it all joy; rejoice in the product of perseverance. You're going to learn perseverance!

You may say, Why do I need perseverance? Perseverance is an action word, a faith-action word. That which causes depression many times in your life is when you don't do anything! God is not in the habit of sending trials—God allows trials to come into your life, and through that trial He brings about a test of your character to prove your genuineness. The principle is this: Rejoice that God is going to use that trial that has come into your life to refine you into a more Christ-like person—to build more character in you. Rejoice in the product of the trial, not in the trial itself. You will find it difficult to discover a place in the Bible where God explains the cause or the why of the many trials. What He is most concerned about is what *you* are going to do in response to it.

When you need a faith lift, when trials are in your life, refocus. Refocus first of all by rejoicing in the product, knowing that the testing of your faith produces perseverance. You know the same kind of thing is seen in athletics. You go through the pain so that you can hang onto the product. I don't know anyone in athletics who likes whistle drills. I don't know of anybody in athletics who gets excited about running the laps. But in athletics we go through the pain so we can enjoy the product. It is the same kind of principle. Focus on the product—rejoice in it!

"And let perseverance have its perfect result, that you may be perfect (mature), lacking in nothing." The product of perseverance will move you toward your goal of maturity and completeness. Rejoice in that product because of its positive results.

An interesting and appropriate verse in the Bible which amplifies the reason for rejoicing in the outcome of trials is: "And we know that God causes all things to work together for good to those who love God, to those who are called according to His purpose" (Romans 8:28). It is not saying that everything that comes into your life is good. It's saying that *He will work all things together for good.* You have a tragedy that comes into your life, and that tragedy in and of itself is bad. Don't ever let anybody teach you that Christianity says that tragedy is good. It is not good! When my mother died, that was a tragedy in my own life. When my father died, that was a tragedy in my own life. I am not excited about the fact that my parents died. That bothers me. I do not like that which was not good, but together with something else it brought about good *for me.* We know that *all* things—every piece of garbage that comes into your life, every little irritation throughout the day you face, every circumstance that gets you down—God will cause to work *together* with something else for the purpose of good.

God will use that trial (no matter the cause) to make you a better person—a more valuable person. The trial that you experience—divorce, bankruptcy, abortion, rape, death of a loved one, disease—could move you toward intense loneliness with all its pain. But there is an alternative. You can find the handle on that same potentially destructive trial and respond properly to it. This builds a quality into your own life and enables you to empathize and counsel with others who experience the same kinds of trials.

We know that God causes all things to work together for good to those who love God, to those who are called according to His purpose, to those who are plugged into an active relationship with God.

Rejoicing in the product can move you to a state of maturity where you will be lacking in nothing. "But if any of you lacks wisdom, let him ask of God, who gives to all men generously and without reproach, and it will be given to him. But let him ask in faith, without any doubting, for the one who doubts is like the surf of the sea, driven and tossed by the wind. For let not that man expect that he will receive anything from the Lord, being a double-minded man, unstable in all his ways." This is a promise that I think is the most exciting promise that I know in the Bible, primarily because I am involved in trials a lot of the time. It seems like the longer I live and the more I do, the more trials I get into. "If any of you lacks wisdom at a time like this, let him ask of God."

Request a New Perspective

When you are under the pile and this trial is overwhelming you, there is a second action step after you rejoice in the product: *Request a new perspective*—ask for wisdom. Pray for wisdom. Pray for God's kind of wisdom, "who gives to all men generously and without reproach, and it will be given to him." If you ask for wisdom, you will get it. It is not saying that if you ask for a way out, it will be given to you. It's not saying that if you want an escape hatch, it will be shown to you. It's saying that God will give you wisdom to figure it out! Isn't that interesting! God does not take over and operate us as robots. He says, "I want you to ask for wisdom, so that you will figure out what would be the wisest thing to do to move through it." But notice how you are supposed to ask: "But let him ask in faith, without any doubting, for the one who doubts is like the surf of the sea, driven and tossed by the wind."

"The surf of the sea driven" is to be blown horizontally, and "tossed by the wind" is a rippling effect where you are bobbing up and down in the water. You are being driven this way and that way and are bobbing up and down. That's being really mixed up! If you doubt when asking for wisdom, then you will be aimless, confused, mised-up, and disoriented.

"For let not that man expect that he will receive anything from the Lord, being a double-minded man, unstable in all his ways." There is a good book that talks about doubt called *In Two Minds*. The title itself is a good definition of doubt—*In Two Minds*. The Chinese have an expression that describes when you are in doubt. It's when you have one foot attempting to step down into two boats. That is indecision. That is doubt! The English say that you've got one foot in each camp. But the main idea is that you are in two minds; you don't know which way to go; you're between disbelief and belief. God says that when you ask for wisdom, ask in faith, and God will give you wisdom. It's asking Him for wisdom and He will give it to you. Count on it!

When you need a faith lift, when you are under the pile of trials, just don't lie there. Don't roll over and play dead. Don't wait for God to bail you out. Do something! *Refocus by rejoicing in the product and by requesting a new perspective.* "No temptation has overtaken you but such as is common to man; and God is faithful, who will not allow you to be tempted beyond what you are able, but with the temptation will provide the way of escape also, that you may be able to endure it" (1 Corinthians 10:13). God allows temptation to take place. He allows trials to come into your life. But this is common to everybody. There is something comforting about knowing that we're going through the same kind of trials as everyone else. There is a real lift in knowing that I'm not the only one who has ever had this problem!

Have you ever been in a trial (maybe you're there now) where you are wondering how much more you can take? With the trial God will provide the way of escape so that you may be able to endure, to persevere! When the circumstances get you down, you don't have to stay down under. There is a mountain pass (a way of escape) to show you how you can get out from under the "insurmountable" circumstances.

Reconsider Your Own Position

When you need a faith lift, rejoice in the product, request a new perspective, and finally *reconsider your own position*. Continuing in the biblical blueprint, "But let the brother of humble circumstances glory in his high position; and let the rich man glory in his humiliation, because like flowering grass he will pass away. For the sun rises with a scorching wind and withers the grass and its flower falls off and the beauty of its appearance is destroyed; so too the rich man in the midst of his pursuits will fade away."

Does a person in poverty have high position?

No, not in this physical world. "But let the brother that lives in the ghetto area glory in his high position"—spiritually. In the eyes of people you look like you are in poverty, you are a lowly person, but in spiritual things you should glory in your high position because you're much higher before God. "And let the rich man glory in his lowly estate because, like flowering grass, he will pass away." Before people, the rich man looks like he is the greatest of all. But before God, in his spiritual state, he is leveled right down with the person who is in poverty. Trials are the great leveler of both rich and poor.

When I sit down with a multimillionaire who is lying back in bed waiting to die, it makes no difference what he's got in material wealth.

When I sit down with a pauper with all his bills, it doesn't make any difference either. Trials are the great leveler of all people. Reconsider your position before God. Refocus by reconsidering your position. When you need a faith lift you must refocus. Refocus by 1) rejoicing in the product, 2) requesting a new perspective, and 3) reconsidering your position before God.

Move Through the Piles

Faith is like a kite: A contrary wind makes it go higher. When circumstances gang up on you and position you in a lonely state, you must make a decision to refocus. When you need a faith lift, you need to refocus. Don't look at the trials, but rejoice in the product, request a new perspective, and reconsider your position spiritually before God. The result? Instead of the circumstantial piles weighting you down, alienating you, and overwhelming you, you'll move through those piles toward life!

CHAPTER NOTES

Chapter 1
Big Brother Isn't Watching

1. "The American Family," in *The Wilson Quarterly*, Summer 1980, p. 116.
2. Suzanne Gordon, *Lonely in America* (New York: Simon and Schuster, 1976), p. 15.
3. Ira J. Tanner, *Loneliness: The Fear of Love* (New York: Harper and Row, 1973), p. IX.
4. Erich Fromm, *The Art of Loving* (Harper and Row, 1956).
5. Elizabeth Skoglund, *Loneliness* (Madison, WI: InterVarsity Press, 1975), p. 33.
6. Tanner, *Loneliness: The Fear of Love*, pp. 90-91.
7. Derek Bowskill, *People Need People* (London: Wildwood House Limited, 1977), p. 2.
8. Gordon, *Lonely in America*, p. 197.
9. Ibid., p. 198.
10. Ibid., p. 284.
11. James J. Lynch, *The Broken Heart* (New York: Basic Books, Inc. 1977), p. 223.
12. Ibid., pp. 192-93.
13. Fritz Perls, *Great Therapy Verbatim* (California: Real People Press, 1969).
14. Gordon, *Lonely in America*, p. 305.
15. Bowskill, *People Need People*, Foreword.
16. Mary Sarton, *Journal of a Solitude*.
17. Erich Fromm, *Man for Himself*.
18. Clark E. Moustakas, *Loneliness and Love* (Englewood Cliffs: Prentice Hall, Inc., 1972), p. 20.
19. Bowskill, *People Need People*, p. 13.
20. Lynch, *Broken Heart*, p. 205.
21. Ibid.

Chapter 2
Middle-Age Crazy

1. Flo Conway and Jim Siegelman, *Snapping* (New York: J.B. Lippincott, 1978), p. 183.
2. Ibid., pp. 184-85.
3. Ibid., p. 154.
4. Gordon Porter Miller, *Life Choices* (New York: Thomas Y. Crowell, 1978), p. 7.
5. Ronald Enroth, *Young Brainwashing and the Extremist Cults* (Grand Rapids: Zondervan, 1977), pp. 149-50.

6.   Miller, *Life Choices*, p. 30.
7.   Conway and Siegelman, *Snapping*, pp. 188-90.
8.   Christopher Lasch, *The Culture of Narcissism* (New York: W.W. Norton & Company, Inc., 1978), p. 199.
9.   Ibid., p. 27.
10. Ibid., p. 30.
11. Ibid., p. 96.
12. Udo Middelmann, *Pro-Existence* (Downers Grove, IL: InterVarsity Press, 1974), p. 14.
13. Conway and Siegelman, *Snapping*, p. 226.
14. Lasch, *Culture*, p. 200.
15. Middelmann, *Pro-Existence*, p. 107.
16. Otto Kernberg, "Why Some People Can't Love," in *Psychology Today*, June 1978, p. 55.
17. Ibid., p. 6.
18. Ibid., pp. 56-57.
19. Ibid., p. 58.
20. Lasch, *Culture*, p. 37.
21. Ibid., p. XVI.
22. William Glasser, *The Identity Society* (New York: Harper & Row, 1976), p. 65.
23. Ibid., pp. 65-66.

Chapter 3
Terrorism Within the Family

1.   "The Battered Wife: What's Being Done?" in *Los Angeles Times*, April 27, 1978.
2.   Lasch, *Culture*, p. 176.
3.   Alvin Toffler, *Future Shock* (New York: Random House, 1970), p. 238.
4.   Ibid., p. 258.
5.   Robert S. Weiss, *Loneliness* (Cambridge: The MIT Press, 1973), p. 90.
6.   Gordon, *Lonely in America*, p. 61.
7.   "Saving the Family," in *Newsweek*, May 15, 1978, pp. 67-68.

Chapter 4
The Pain Can Kill You!

1.   Bowskill, *People Need People*, p. 15.
2.   Glasser, *Identity Society*, p. 43.
3.   Ibid., pp. 43-44.
4.   Ibid., p. 48.
5.   Ibid., p. 68.

6. James J. Lynch & William H. Convey, "Loneliness, Disease, and Death: Alternative Approaches," in reprint from *Psychosomatics*, Oct. 1979.
7. Lynch, *Broken Heart*, p. 3.
8. Ibid., pp. 32, 52.
9. Tanner, *Loneliness: The Fear of Love*, p. 51.
10. Lynch, *Broken Heart*, pp. 81-82.
11. J.J. Groen, "Influence of Sociological and Cultural Patterns of Psychosomatic Diseases," in *Psychother, Psychosm*, 1970, pp. 189-213.
12. Lynch, *Broken Heart*, pp. 158-59.
13. Tanner, *Loneliness: The Fear of Love*, p. 111.

Chapter 5
I'm Not O.K., You're Not O.K., and That's O.K.

1. John Powell, *A Reason to Live—A Reason to Die* (Chicago: Argus Communications, 1972), pp. 35-36.
2. Ibid., p. 37.
3. Ibid., pp. 41-42.
4. Lasch, *Culture*, p. 37.
5. John Powell, *Why Am I Afraid to Love?* (Chicago: Argus Communications, 1972), p. 40.
6. Gordon, *Lonely in America*, p. 19.
7. Bowskill, *People Need People*, p. 22.
8. Skoglund, *Loneliness*, pp. 17-18.
9. Bowskill, *People Need People*, p. 226.
10. Gordon, *Lonely in America*, p. 26.
11. Moustakas, *Loneliness and Love*, p. 68.
12. Skoglund, *Loneliness*, p. 18.
13. Lasch, *Culture*, p. 27.
14. Glasser, *Identity Society*, p. 29.
15. Ibid., p. 30.

Chapter 6
Loneliness Is a Decision

1. Lynch, *Broken Heart*, p. 160.
2. Glasser, *Identity Society*, pp. 55-56.
3. Ibid., p. 57.
4. Tanner, *Loneliness: the Fear of Love*, p. XI.
5. Ibid., pp. 79-80.
6. Ibid., p. 36.
7. Ibid., p. 12.

8.   Moustakas, *Loneliness and Love*, pp. 143-45.
9.   Tanner, *Loneliness: the Fear of Love*, p. X.
10. Moustakas, *Loneliness and Love*, p. 87.
11. Clark E. Moustakas, *The Touch of Loneliness* (Englewood Cliffs, NJ: Prentice-Hall, Inc., 1975), pp. 77-78.
12. Tanner, *Loneliness, the Fear of Love*, p. 71.
13. Powell, *Why Am I Afraid to Love?*, pp. 23-24.

Chapter 7
Pseudolove

1.   John Powell, *Why Am I Afraid to Tell You Who I Am?* (Chicago: Argus Communications, 1969), p. 13.
2.   Marshall Bryant Hodge, *Your Fear of Love* (New York: Dolphin Books, 1967), pp. 3-4.
3.   Powell, *Why . . . Who I Am?*, pp. 43-44.
4.   Hodge, *Your Fear of Love*, p. 106.
5.   John Powell, *The Secret of Staying in Love* (Chicago: Argus Communications, 1974), p. 15.
6.   Ibid., p. 21.
7.   Erich Fromm, *The Art of Loving*.
8.   Powell, *The Secret of Staying in Love*, p. 64.
9.   Bowskill, *People Need People*, p. 227.
10. Ibid.

Chapter 8
True Love

1.   Ed Wheat, *Love Life* (Grand Rapids: Zondervan, 1980), p. 57.
2.   Tim Timmons, *Maximum Living in a Pressure-Cooker World* (Waco: Word Books, 1979), p. 188.
3.   Powell, *Secret*, p. 55.
4.   Ibid., p. 56.
5.   Lewis B. Smedes, *Love Without Limits* (Grand Rapids: Wm. B. Eerdmans, 1978), pp. 1, 11.
6.   Powell, *Secret*, p. 53.
7.   Ibid., pp. 69-70.

Chapter 9
True Love: Release It!

1.   Powell, *Why . . . Who I Am?* chapter 3.

2. Ibid., pp. 56-57.
3. Powell, *Why . . . Afraid to Love?* pp. 100-01.
4. Powell, *Secret*, p. 130.
5. Alan Loy McGinnis, *The Friendship Factor* (Minneapolis: Augsburg Publishing House, 1979), p. 28.
6. Powell, p. 34.
7. Powell, *Why . . . Who I Am?* p. 70.
8. Ibid., p. 74.
9. David Augsburger, *Caring Enough to Confront* (Glendale: Regal Books, 1980), p. 52.
10. Matthew 7:1-5.
11. David Augsburger, *The Freedom of Forgiveness* (Chicago: Moody Press, 1970), p. 13.
12. Judson J. Swihart, *How Do You Say I Love You?* (Downers Grove, IL: InterVarsity Press, 1977), p. 55.
13. Dan Montgomery and Everett L. Shostrom, *Healing Love* (New York: Bantam Books, 1979), p. 87.
14. McGinnis, *Friendship*, p. 86.
15. Ibid., p. 89.
16. William Backus and Marie Chapian, *Telling Yourself the Truth* (Minneapolis: Bethany Fellowship, Inc., 1980), p. 142.
17. Powell, *Secret*, p. 13.

Appendix I.
Perfect Love

1. Augsburger, *Freedom of Forgiveness*, pp. 73-74.
2. Matthew 22:36-40.
3. 1 John 4:7.
4. 1 John 4:8-19.
5. Romans 8:35,37-39.
6. 1 John 4:20,21.
7. John 21:15-17.